SECRETS OF THE OCCULT

Secrets
OF THE Occult

C A Burland

Ebury Press London

First published 1972 by Ebury Press
Chestergate House Vauxhall Bridge Road London SW1V 1HF

Copyright © Text C. A. Burland 1972

Made by Roxby Press Productions
55 Conduit Street London W1R 9FD
Editor Tony Aspler
Picture research: Anne Horton : Ann Davies
Design and art direction Ivan and Robin Dodd

Printed in Great Britain by Oxley Press Limited

ISBN: 0 85223 023 0

CONTENTS

. . . . let not men say
'These are their reasons-they are natural'
For I believe they are portentous things

JULIUS CAESAR Act 1 Scene 3 *Shakespeare*

Twentieth-century man is a mass of paradoxes. As the year 2000 looms ahead our technology has turned ancient myth into reality: men walk on the Moon; images from the other side of the world reach us in seconds – yet the more science helps us to understand our world, the more we look for answers elsewhere, from the world of the spirit and the study of the occult. Universal education may have dispelled our fears of witchcraft and dissipated our prejudice against fortune-tellers but our fascination for dark, forbidden secrets remains.

Chapter One

FROM *Now* TILL *Then*

Today witches both black and white appear on television. In newspapers astrologers are compulsively read by men and women whose instincts for the mysterious are stronger than the materialism of the age. Society today tolerates the existence of occultist groups whose practices would have led their forefathers through the torture chamber to the gallows or the stake and then to an unmarked grave at a crossroads. Offbeat religious sects now flourish all over the world. There are groups, like the Church of the Final Judgment, who believe that God and Satan are one and the same force; and societies exist like the followers of the Rosy Cross, who, as innocently as Freemasons, conduct mysterious

rituals to help one another in their stated aims. Spiritual healers have become the last resort where medical science fails. When Christianity no longer provides spiritual nourishment believers seek God through magical incantations or ecstatic dancing like that of the Brazilian Macumba, West Indian Pocomania, or the group in the south-eastern United States whose devotees dance with rattlesnakes.

At no time in the history of civilization has occultism in its various forms been so widely practised as it is today. Dedicated groups dabble in the Black Arts, perhaps only to release the tensions of modern life by breaking accepted social norms. Yet we live in an era of cold scientific logic. To a greater or lesser degree, however, this strange dichotomy has always existed. Today it is only more dramatically defined.

The quest for the supernatural is probably a flight from the desperation of the age – a search for novelty, part of a pattern of rejection of accepted religious beliefs in the western world. The mystical religions of the east are attracting many young people away from Christianity. The ordinary every-day patterns of worship have lost their mystery to a generation brought up on the disciplines of

left Hands as the vehicle of power. Members of a coven project energy through physical contact which can be directed at will to convey ideas by telepathy.

left Religion and magic in Victorian England. Even inside the church one sees tokens of primitive nature worship in the decorative shrubs.

left A contemporary coven performs the traditional circle-dance around the fire. The 'cone of power' created can be directed by the will of the leader.
below Within the charmed circle, marked with the symbols and names of the Supreme Being, the priestess directs power generated by the members of the coven.

above Mrs Bone, a well known leader in English witchcraft circles, pronounces an invocation over a magical cauldron.

the state religion. Today the Church has to compete with secular entertainments which poach upon its preserve. Rock musicals like 'Jesus Christ Superstar' and 'Godspell' create their own followings, ignoring the traditional religious hierarchy and making them unfashionable. In an attempt to combat this kind of apostasy, the Church sometimes tries to reconcile its traditional religious practices with the popular secular custom. Christian apologists may try to appeal to rationalist minds by explaining religion as an inspired myth, and fundamentalists may thunder against the Church service turned circus, yet both would consider themselves in touch with the supernatural power of Divinity. But so too, by their own definitions, would the rattlesnake dancers of America.

Behind these conflicting and contradictory viewpoints there is a basic clash between, on the one hand, the sceptic whose materialist mind refuses to allow him to believe in anything he cannot experience through his senses and, on the other, those who are willing to allow that supernatural forces do exist – perhaps the majority of mankind.

Our concept of the supernatural keeps changing; science as it marches forward leaves old, discarded notions in its wake. What was once feared as the magic of witches and sorcerers – electricity, magnetism and hypnosis, for example – is now taken for granted. But modern science has still to fathom those phenomena for which there are no rational explanations: dreams foretelling future events, ghosts that have appeared to too many people to be discounted, or the contention of spiritualists that matter has passed through matter – an object has been seen moving through the wall of a room and has felt warm on arrival! Even the uncanny but common sensation of having seen a place before though we have never visited it, or of hearing a conversation which has already been heard in the mind, these kinds of experiences are sufficient to arouse our curiosity about the supernatural and with it our desire to lift the veil of mystery that surrounds our waking hours.

Some take up the study of the occult out of curiosity alone. Some take comfort for their own mortality by seeking messages from beyond the grave. And, significantly, some will try to advance themselves in their chosen careers by joining a witch coven. (The word 'coven', incidentally, is a corruption of 'convent'.) At these gatherings the participants might dance in a circle to project a 'cone of power' or influence, a kind of telepathy that can affect other people's minds at a distance. Through such ceremonies they hope to increase their inner power and thus further their own ambitions.

This idea of self-advancement through supernatural forces is an important part of the attraction of the occult. We become frustrated by the straight-jacket of conformity, by all the rules and disciplines that a sophisticated society imposes upon us. Our natural pattern of behaviour is inhibited by the real or imagined walls we build around ourselves and we yearn to get back to a life closer to our instincts. Some of these instincts are served by the sexual aspects of occultism which acts as a liberating force channelling pent-up feelings into a natural outlet. Most witch covens practice their rituals naked, and initiation rites usually centre around some aspect of fertility worship, though nowadays they are less 'abandoned' than in the past.

This ritualized catharsis – a kind of sexual safety valve – is important to witchcraft. Witches emphasize that the purpose of their rituals is to promote the well-being of the initiate and the coven in the sense that each participant becomes united with the powers of nature, in tune with the Life Force – the elemental need of man as well as all other life forms on our planet.

Since man's natural state is nakedness, members abandon their clothes to atune themselves to the rhythms of life and to celebrate the mysteries of sex. What their critics condemn as orgiastic and licentious they experience as a new and more harmonious balance of personality. This concept of man's relationship to organic life has a direct link with primitive religions.

above The Rollright Stones. This circle of stones in Oxfordshire, England, dates back to the second millenium BC. It was originally used to determine the divisions of the solar year.
right The White Mare of the Dobunni carved on a hill crest in the Berkshire Downs. The chalk carving represented the Celtic moon goddess Epona.

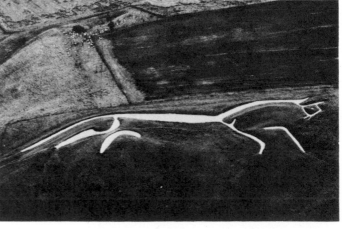

above Fifteenth- and sixteenth-century impressions of witchcraft.
upper right Witches flying with the Demon on a magic broom cause a destructive hail-storm.
upper left A horned Devil seizes a witch from her home and carries her off to perdition.
centre A group of Italian witches, protected within their magic circle, meet the Devil.

The public attitude towards witchcraft is one of baffled disapproval. From time to time the Press regales us with lurid stories of drug-taking and seductions at witches' sabbaths, of tombstones desecrated and graves robbed of skulls for magic circles. In fact, whenever a tomb is broken into, the popular assumption is that witch groups have been at work. The public condemnation of witches is tinged with suppressed envy for the supposed erotic pleasures taken by naked witches indulging in orgiastic dances.

Given such an image, it is hardly surprising that witches don't go about advertising for new members. They prefer to recruit from among friends whom they can trust to be discreet. Prospective initiates are put through tests which tell them little of the coven's doings. The more extreme groups which use Eleusinian rites are purposely more secretive since their initiation rituals involve the exposing of a rotting corpse. (The Eleusians buried a pig and a year later dug up its decaying corpse as a symbolic demonstration that all flesh is mortal.) On the other hand, since witchcraft is no longer illegal witches enjoy relative security to the point where they can actively seek new members if they so wish. The Gardnerian covens – the disciples of Gerald Gardner – used publicity to popularize the practice of witchcraft. (In the 1950s Gardner himself used to encourage members of the Press to report his meetings.) Some covens have even registered and been accepted as legitimate religious groups, and one coven has even gone as far as putting on a stage presentation of their rituals to attract new members.

Yet the majority of traditional witches and occultists have kept themselves apart and have remained exclusive societies who shun publicity. The result is that those not within the fold either dismiss them as cranks or suspect the worst. Fortunately in our enlightened times most people consider it merely amusing that a group of their respectable acquaintances should cavort naked in a suburban sitting-room on the eve of a full moon.

Some covens still survive which have a genuine background of folk-tradition. Long-established assemblies of witches can trace participating members of their families for three generations, and some as far back as the seventeenth century. Such groups have no use for clamorous publicity, no need to proselytize, and certainly no wish to arouse the suspicion and hatred of their neighbours. They remind themselves of the great witch-trials three hundred years ago when tens of thousands of their co-practitioners were burned or hanged all over Europe. For England one estimate covering the reign of James I alone was 70,000

above The Roman Emperor Marcus Aurelius prepares to sacrifice an ox in honour of the gods of Rome (161–180 AD).

above St Giles celebrating Holy Mass before Charles Martel, King of France. The Angel bears a scroll inscribed with the King's sins. By the Master of St Giles, *c.* fifteenth century.

witches hanged! (King James at first disbelieved the confessions made by witches under torture until one of the accused, a certain Agnes Sampson 'declared unto him the verye woordes which passed betweene the Kings Maiestie and his Queen at Upslo in Norway the first night of their marriage, with their answere eache to other. . . .' Declaring that 'all the Devils in hell could not have discovered the same, acknowledging her woords to be most true', James became an ardent supporter of witch prosecutions and even published a treatise on the subject, entitled 'Daemonologie'.)

Since even the most tolerant of societies are unpredictable in their attitudes towards extra-social activities like witchcraft, members have to be very careful about their initiation ceremonies. Such evidence that we have of these ritual initiations is hardly sensational: a prospective member is turned loose in a field at night and is quietly observed by other members unknown to him. The idea is to observe how the 'new boy' reacts to nature. Hardly immoral, although in most modern groups there are cases where new members are tied up, blindfolded and beaten.

In his book *The History of Witchcraft and Demonology*, Father Montague Summers contended that 'Modern Spiritism is merely Witchcraft revived'. Certainly the current fashion for occultism owes much to past practices. A particular influence on several contemporary groups has been a charming little book entitled *Aradia*, written a century ago by Charles Godfrey Leland about the witches of Tuscany and giving accounts of ceremonies and chants, many of which have been used by modern occultists. But there are great gaps in our knowledge of traditional coven practices; the threat of torture and death for anyone found guilty of indulging in witchcraft, a threat which lasted until the eighteenth century, ensured that the ceremonies would remain secret and jealously guarded.

Even men of science were regarded by the superstitious imagination of the Middle Ages as necromancers and Devil-worshippers. Friar Roger Bacon's experiments with gunpowder in the thirteenth century outraged the populace who were convinced that he dealt in black magic, calling up demons to help him in his workshop. He was also thought to have fashioned a brazen head capable of speech. This same accusation had been levelled against Bishop Gerbert of Aurillac, later Pope Sylvester II, two hundred and fifty years earlier for his inventions and for his possession of a special form of clock. If the most brilliant minds of the Middle Ages were suspected of trafficking with the Devil then old women who lived alone and collected herbs

and roots to perform medical spells were all the more open to the charge. Secrecy was the only form of self-protection. Even within the coven, the elders were loath to pass on the more esoteric aspects of their cult.

Persecution of witches reached frightening proportions at the end of the Middle Ages, spurred on by the intellectual turmoil of the Renaissance. In earlier times the Church in England, for example, accepted folk-ceremonies whose roots go back to the primitive Celtic religions: ceremonies such as the scrubbing of the Hill figures (the White Horse cut into the chalk of the Berkshire Downs, the Giant at Cerne Abbas in Dorset, and the Long Man of Wilmington in Sussex) and Morris dancing and maypoles. These ceremonies took place in daylight with public approval, and were countenanced by the Church which could not suppress them. By the same token, perhaps, they only hanged witches and occultists for specific crimes such as murder and open blasphemy, and not for any covert ritual practices.

There has never been a time since history was first recorded when man has not dabbled in some form of occult practice. In certain ages its practitioners met violent ends, hated and abused by ignorant and fearful neighbours who in other times would have raised them to the level of the gods they worshipped. Man's thirst for secret knowledge began when he realized that the forces of nature were stronger than himself, and all around the world we find evidence of primeval man's search for knowledge through the worship of nature.

Looking back through history we have ample evidence of a variety of occult practices which would suggest that the roots of magic grow deep in the hearts of men. In Julius Caesar's Rome witches experimented with love-philtres and poisons, and if occasionally the two were inadvertently mixed the hapless 'chemist' met her end at the hands of the mob. While witches were defamed in the streets prophets and priests practised their own magic inside their temples, protected and indeed revered within the framework of the state religion as they spoke with the illustrious dead or called down the wrath of Jupiter on their enemies.

The cultured Greeks before them celebrated Bacchanalian revels of terrifying excess in which animals were torn apart by intoxicated followers of Dionysus. The same dualism existed in the midst of the Babylonians who dreaded demons and the sorceresses they believed were in league with them. Yet on entering their temples they looked for omens and consulted the stars. In Ancient

Egypt the high priest and priestess, representing the god and goddess Osiris and Isis, copulated in a ceremonially prepared bed surrounded by temple servants, to ensure the fertility of the life-giving waters of the Nile. They also cast spells over the ushabti figurines, little pottery figures buried with the mummy to act as servants of the dead and rescue them from the necessity of having to hoe the heavenly fields.

In England, Stonehenge, along with the other megalithic monuments of Europe, probably had religious importance. It dates from the second millenium BC and is now thought to be the world's first computer or at least a calendar for making precise astrological calculations. To the twentieth-century mind this places the star-gazers of Stonehenge in the category of scientists. But the ancient world did not make the distinction between science, religion, and magic. To them the towering circle of Stonehenge would have been an amalgam of all three.

The activities of the priest-scientists who computed the passage of the stars at Stonehenge would be largely incomprehensible to the mind of the common man. We can safely assume that he had his own simpler, possibly more ancient cults. Centuries later the religion of the Druids dominated Northern Europe. Today its modern revivalists claim that Stonehenge was its original shrine. The evidence is slight, but there may be a connection between Celtic Druidism and the megalithic circle.

But Stonehenge was a late construction when we consider the Old Stone Age cave-paintings in France and Northern Spain which date back some 30,000 years. These magical pictures of food-animals and wild beasts still keep their secrets. Perhaps the same belief which is prevalent among the North American Indians moved primitive man to paint them: many of the creatures are stuck with a kind of dart and there is an elephant with a specially painted heart, images which suggest that these were so painted to persuade Mother Nature – who makes the souls of the animals in the depths of the earth – to create more food for mankind. The very location of these paintings seems significant. The deep cave was not the home of early man but it symbolized for him the womb of Mother Earth. Even within the caves certain sites appear to be specially sacred – where pictures are superimposed over each other by successive artists while neighbouring surfaces remain untouched. It was not every tribesman who would have the courage and daring in those primeval days to descend into the bowels of the earth with only a tiny lamp made of a wick burning in a bowl of animal fat. Such shrines, the

secret vaults of the Life Force, were probably for initiates only and the rituals conducted there may well have been for common good; but to the uninitiated tribesman they would have been awesome and mysterious places. Thus, at the very beginning of man's magical past, we find the split between the religion of the people and the hidden practices of the priest or initiate, for, looking back over 30,000 years we can only assume that those Stone Age cave artists were the magician-priests of their tribe – the forefathers of a host of magicians and sorcerers who succeeded them – the self-same magicians who during their lifetimes left echoes of the supernatural in the minds of men.

below The Venus of Willendorf, carved 30,000 years ago by an Aurignacian artist. Her ample shape symbolizes the desire of primitive hunters to bring home sufficient food to fatten their womenfolk.

The earliest magician known to us can be seen in the caves of Trois Frères in France. For thousands of years he was hidden from the eyes of men until the cave and its paintings were discovered in the last century. The painting depicts a dancing man wearing a deer-mask. On nearby walls are pictures of exquisite bison, cows and beautiful fat ponies, wide-eyed and savage, perhaps not unlike the hunters who tracked them and killed them for meat, but who loved them nevertheless as fellow creatures of Mother Nature. We have no idea whether the dancing figure represented a real animal-charmer whose dance would mesmerize the wild beasts and draw them nearer for the tribe to kill. Perhaps he was the artist's impression of a natural spirit being, the horned father of the animals, like the Celtic god Cernunnos, the horned creator of life and wisdom – known as the Lord of the Centre. What the sorcerer-musician does tell us is that our remote ancestors believed in a strange occult force which was part of nature and able to command the natural powers.

Man's reliance on the forces of nature increased when he learned how to cultivate the land and grow food for himself, instead of living the life of the wandering hunter. From man's ability to grow his food developed a cult centering on the powers of fertility in the plant world. This in turn led to an interest in astronomy: the early farmers knew well enough when their grain was ripe but, except for the position of the stars in the heavens, they had no natural sign that told them when to plant for the new season.

As astronomy became important as a guide to the communities so too did the men who were selected to watch the stars. A division was created among the religious leaders. Some became star-watchers while others became healers and prophets, whose task it was to seek out and expel the demons which caused sickness. The ceremony and incantations built up to cure illness were no doubt augmented by drugs extracted from roots and herbs by the healer who experimented with them on his patients. It was his duty, too, to keep in contact with the spirits of nature to ensure the fertility of his tribe and the land they worked. The Shaman of primitive Siberian religion and his counterpart among the American Indians (who dances with his magic drum and whose soul, when he falls into a trance, flies from his body to commune with the spirit world) are

Chapter Two

Old gods AND New

arguably the ancestors of today's farm specialists and doctors!

The star-watchers were man's first scientists. They dictated the times of planting and harvesting; they organized ceremonies at the appropriate season of the year so that men should always keep in contact with the powers of nature. The first great astronomers who have left us traces of their knowledge and magic were the Sumerians and their Semitic neighbours in Iraq who believed the bowl of heaven was supported by the mountains beyond the sea. Their long accounts of the gods and the signs in the sky may still be read from inscribed clay tablets that are five thousand years old.

The Sumerians first named the twelve signs of the Zodiac and recorded the eclipses of the sun and moon. They used their knowledge to predict events as well as time the passage of the seasons for the farmers. But alongside evidence of these highly scientific activities we find small clay cursing tablets inscribed with the name of the person to be 'favoured' with demoniacal visitations – very much in the vein of curses recorded in the Old Testament. This suggests that another class of magician was operating as part of the community – one which cast spells to set evil spirits on its enemies to destroy them and their property.

Already it is possible to see that occultism has two faces: one practical, communal and aimed at the common good; the other secret, anti-social and reaching down to the powers of darkness.

To the Egyptian civilization two or three thousand years before our era, astronomy as practised by the priests was an important part of the fertility cult. The priests watched for the rising of Sirius, the brightest of all fixed stars and the sign of the goddess Isis, just as the sun rose which occurred about the time of the summer solstice. The appearance of this brilliant star on the horizon in the morning sky meant that the Nile would rise bringing new life to the whole valley. The annual rise and flooding of the river was an occasion of prayer and rejoicing, the natural order had been preserved for yet another year by the agency of the gods.

Probably no other people has created such a pantheon of gods, goddesses, sacred beings and holy objects as did the Egyptians. In their devotions to the gods they put great store by the magical power of certain words and sounds, like the utterance of the name of the god by the priests – in the same way that the Judaeo-Christian Creator had brought the world into being by uttering the Word. (In Judaism, too, we find another example of the same idea: the name of JHVH was too sacred to be used in writing or prayer and was only uttered by the High Priest on The Day of Atonement, alone in the Holy of Holies.

The Egyptian people wore amulets and charms of wood, stone and pottery. The state itself was under the magical control of the Pharaoh who performed the necessary rituals for the national Life Force in his position as the Divine Son of Ra, the Sun god. This entailed intercourse with a priestess representing Isis, the spirit of the land.

The Temple priests who served the greater gods were all expected to be wonder-workers. An Egyptian papyrus of the XVIII Dynasty (around the time of Tutankhamun) tells the story of how a priest helped a young girl to recover her gold amulet by conjuring half the water of a Temple lake to stand up on the other half so that the girl could recover her precious jewellery without getting her feet wet! But the priests of the Temple did not have a monopoly on the magic arts and we have accounts of the trial of two unscrupulous tomb robbers who used magic to help them perform their nefarious deeds. Found guilty of such acts, criminal magicians were, as was the custom, either strangled or thrown to the crocodiles.

above A Babylonian commemorative stela. At the top are symbols of Shamash the sun god, Sin the moon god and Nergal the storm god. (Ninth century BC.)

right The 'Magician' of the Trois Frères in France. This dancer dating back 30,000 years may either be a magician charming the spirits of the wild deer or a representation of the power of male fertility.

left An American Indian shaman performing a ritual dance to invoke the help of the spirit world on behalf of the young chief seated in front of him. Mandan tribe of the Upper Missouri River. (Ninth to eleventh century BC.)
below Babylonian clay model of a sheep's liver. It is divided into sections – from each an omen can be read. (Ninth to eleventh century BC.)

left An American Indian shaman performing a ritual dance to invoke the help of the spirit world on behalf of the young chief seated in front of him. Mandan tribe of the Upper Missouri River. (Ninth to eleventh century BC.)
below Babylonian clay model of a sheep's liver. It is divided into sections – from each an omen can be read. (Ninth to eleventh century BC.)

Inevitably the advanced culture of the Egyptians affected its neighbours. Belief in prophecy and magic had already implanted itself in the Israelites who worked as slaves in Egypt. In the Book of Exodus we find Moses competing with Pharoah's court magicians in changing their staffs into serpents and surpassing them with the plagues and death of the firstborn by the power given to him by the One God. The ultimate magic, however, was that which ensured Israel's freedom: the parting of the Red Sea and the drowning of Pharaoh's pursuing hosts.

The frequent references to witches in the Bible (especially 'Thou shalt not suffer a witch to live' [Exodus xxii, 18] which was used as a justification for the persecution of witches throughout the centuries) suggests that witchcraft was widely practised in Palestine in biblical times. In the Book of Samuel we read of Saul, Palestine's first anointed king, visiting the Witch of Endor in his desperation at the sight of the Philistine hordes. Saul, a deeply religious man had prohibited on pain of death all practice of magic, yet finding no guidance from God or the prophets turned to 'a

woman that had a familiar spirit'. Through the medium of this woman the disguised Saul spoke to the ghost of Samuel who recognized him immediately and foretold him of his defeat and death.

Looking more closely at the story, it seems clear that in spite of Saul's proscription banishing magicians from the land, the Israelites had secretly supported the Witch of Endor and it was not very difficult for the king to find his way at night to her seance room. Saul's action summed up the rather schizophrenic attitude of the Jews: they subscribed to the disciplines of the Temple Priesthood while still yearning for the fleshly pleasures of the Canaanite religions, particularly the orgiastic worship of the fertility goddess Astarte. The compelling attraction of the magical fertility cult competing against the rational pursuit of a monotheistic religion (the doctrine that there is only one God) run like twin threads through man's history.

Between 1400 and 1100 BC the western Mediterranean witnessed the collision of ancient civilizations with agressive new races. Older nations like the Hittites and the Canaanites were suddenly confronted by intelligent vigorous races like the Greeks, who marched in from the Danube Basin, and the Keftiu from western Asia who settled in Crete. These new races brought with them their own spiritual beliefs, and when they eventually fused they created a complex of independent city-states in which

above Egyptian written charm of the twelfth century BC. For use against headaches and migraine.

philosophy and literature blossomed in spite of the political chaos. Thus began the mighty Greek civilization.

In the sixth century BC the Greek philosopher Pythagoras, a native of Samos, founded a brotherhood at Crotona in Italy where he expounded his ideas on the mathematical basis of the universe. Although the brotherhood was suppressed on suspicion of political activity, Pythagorean students spread their master's teaching that all things depended on number and form. Pythagoras conceived numbers spacially – they had a quality that made them perfect, being free from the corruption of the flesh and the imperfections of the senses. Numbers were symmetrical, the Logos in them was a pattern. So Pythagoras deduced that anything capable of being measured had reached a state of near perfection; whereas something that could not be brought to rational order by measuring was in a comparatively primitive state and therefore evil. Here Pythagoras was reinterpreting the early Babylonian creation myth in terms of his own rational philosophy.

Many of Pythagoras's ideas were no doubt common knowledge among Mediterranean peoples of his time, but he systematized them into the study of geometry and reduced its principles to a formal unity. Alongside this rational approach to the universe Pythagoreans evolved a mystical doctrine of numbers: the Good was one, which meant unity; Justice was four, the next square number, and so on. Here we see the beginnings of the mystical power invested in numbers, especially in the belief in symbolic numerical squares in which each column of numbers whether added vertically, horizontally or diagonally resulted in the same figure. These squares reflected the structure of the universe and would have been to Pythagoras what atomic diagrams are to modern scientists.

If the ideas of Pythagoras created a system in which his followers could find deep religious as well as scientific meaning, they also provided in their debased, second-hand usage a kind of magic. The numerical squares and triangles by which Pythagoras had proved that there was order in the universe were taken over by the uneducated and worn as charms. The musings of the pre-Socratic philosophers had little impact on the Greek masses who distrusted the new rationalism and continued to pray to the ritual gods.

Apart from the pagan rites of the state religion the most famous of Greek religious ceremonies were the Eleusinian Mysteries – a cult from which all but the initiated were excluded. Around the ancient Mycenaean site at Eleusis, near Athens, the rites of the goddess Demeter and her daughter Persephone were celebrated at harvest time. These

above Ancient Egyptian double-looped girdle of Isis. This magical knot was a symbol of unity and strength.
right The prophet Moses demonstrates the divine power by changing a rod into a serpent before the Pharaoh and his court. A nineteenth-century reproduction.

mysteries were an echo of earlier agrarian festivals and from the little we know of the ritual it appears to have been a feast of purification and fertility before the corn was sown. Grafted on to the myth was the idea of the lower world – Persephone's abduction by Pluto into Hades – and life after death. Legend has it that the cult of Demeter was introduced to Eleusis in the fifteenth century BC. 'Then Demeter went, and to the kings who deal justice . . .' wrote Homer, 'she showed the conduct of her rites and taught them all her mysteries . . . awful mysteries which no one may in any way transgress and pry into or utter, for deep awe of the gods checks the voice'.

Anyone found guilty of divulging the secrets of the cult was severely punished, cursed or even killed. So effective was the wall of silence around the Mysteries that we know little today of the rituals. Among the secrets which did escape are a few broad details of the initiation ceremonies: initiates were placed in a darkened maze; they witnessed a mystery play about the King Triptolemos who was ordered by Demeter to travel the world and teach mankind how to cultivate grain; seated on thrones and dressed in lambskins they watched an enactment of the divine mating of the gods; and at the climax, in a darkened hall, the worshippers were shown visions in flashes of light.

The effect of these rites on the initiates was, according to all accounts, visible for all to see as they returned from the Temple in joyful procession. Spiritually uplifted and filled with new life and purpose, they returned to their homes and worked to enrich the lives of lesser mortals – for there was great social prestige in being selected for initiation.

The popularity of the Eleusinian Mysteries lasted well into Roman times and, one hundred years before Christ, Cicero tells us of the special veneration surrounding the worship of Demeter; 'Nothing is higher than those Mysteries. They have sweetened our characters and softened our customs; they have made us pass from the condition of savages to true humanity, but they have taught us how to die with a better hope.'

In contrast to the ennobling effects of the Eleusinian Mysteries was the licence and blood-frenzy generated by

left Part of the Eleusinian mystery tradition : Demeter, the goddess, blesses Triptolemos in his winged chariot prior to his journey round the world to bring the gift of grain.

above From the Villa of the Mysteries, Pompeii. The mother meditates, the boy plays hymns to Demeter and the maid-servant carries a tray of honey cakes – the sacred food of the underworld.

above Io Dionysio ! The vine-wreathed Lord of the Dance, and the terrible powers of Nature. From a coin of Nazos, Sicily, before 480 BC.
left A herm of Dionysus from Greek North Africa. The god of wine was regarded as a source of inspiration and frenzy as described in Euripides' 'The Bacchae'.

the worship of Dionysus. As Demeter taught men to grow corn so Dionysus taught men the culture of the vine, and his rites are of equal antiquity. The god of wine came from the east to Thebes to establish his worship in Greece, bringing the vine and accompanied by a train of frenzied women dancing and singing exultant songs, wearing fawn-skins over their robes and waving ivy-bound wands.

The arrival of this foreign deity was at first regarded with suspicion by the elders of Greek society, especially when they saw the results of his benedictions – the corruption of the young. Just as wine has two natures – in moderation 'the merry-maker' bringing fun and gaiety; in excess man's destroyer – so, too, did the god. Homer describes him as 'he whose locks are bound with gold, Ruddy Bacchus', and as the heartless, brutal god who 'hunts his prey, snares and drags him to his death with his Bacchanals'.

But to younger Greeks the cult of Dionysus was seductive in its abandon, offering its celebrants a total surrender to the powers of nature. By consuming as much wine as possible the followers of the god – the Satyrs and Maenads – thought that they could themselves become divine. Their excesses led to orgies of blood as they raced through the woods threatening the life of anything that crossed their paths. Under the drunken power of the god they would tear apart animals and even human beings. When the effects of the wine wore off the votaries would return home at peace with themselves and content with the glorious memory of having danced with the god.

Euripides in his tragedy 'The Bacchae' describes the two aspects of the cult – the glory and the terror. Pentheus, the King of Thebes, orders the imprisonment of the strange women and their leader 'whose face is flushed with wine, a cheating sorcerer from Lydia'. The blind prophet Tiresias tries to warn the king but to no avail, and the god is bound and imprisoned. His followers escape to the hills, where they are joined by many Theban women, among them Pentheus's mother. When Pentheus sets out to pursue them the god enrages the women; they mistake the king for a mountain lion and tear him limb from limb.

Imperial Rome worshipped Jupiter and a galaxy of lesser gods, and when the legions raised their banners over Europe and the eastern Mediterranean they carried their religion with them. Inside the boundaries of the empire for over four hundred years the Roman Imperial religion triumphed over foreign deities by force of arms. Local religions were tolerated as long as their gods were roughly equivalent to Roman ones (for instance, the German

Wotan who resembled Mercury). Two religions however were proscribed by Rome: Judaism because the God of Israel would tolerate no other gods, and Druidism which venerated the oak and the mistletoe and was not above human sacrifice at the end of the old year and the beginning of the new – the time of our All Hallows festivals.

Within an otherwise tolerant Roman society quasi-religious groups began to mushroom – burial societies, trade guilds whose members worshipped a particular god, and associations which glorified annual events such as the Lupercalia, when the priests ran around the city striking every woman they met – an action designed to make them fruitful! The various groups had something of the nature of secret fraternity designed to bring together and assist like-minded people – the Roman equivalent of today's Freemasons. Even the Roman masses were involved in these societies and some of the early Christians set up clandestine places of worship under the guise of state-registered burial societies.

Among the more important of these groups were the military cults of the Invincible Sun and of Mithras. Mithras was one of the chief gods of Persia later identified with the sun. According to myth, by slaying the great bull which symbolized the universe, Mithras brought light and life into being. He was worshipped in a small building with an apse in which stood a statue of the god slaying a bull. He is generally represented as a young man wearing a Phrygian

below Maenad and Satyr. A terracotta relief expressing the gaiety of the dance in the wildwood. The erotic nature of this dance culminated in such frenzy that participants tore to pieces any living creature which crossed their path.

left The Roman God Aion embossed with zodiacal signs. A divine being of creation and destruction whose image stood in every temple of Mithras. (Second century AD.)

ass's heads, which may have allowed junior officers, in their roles as priests of Mithras, to order about their superiors without embarrassment or tension.

To the political powers in Rome these army cults were highly acceptable since they fostered the military virtues and placed great store by loyalty and devotion to duty. Inevitably, the practice of the Mithraic rites and other military-religious cults spread to wherever units of the army were posted about the empire. Later on, the tests of courage which initiates into the Mithraic rites had to undergo were maintained through the Secret Societies of the Middle Ages and among the Rosicrucians, in the form of trials and penances.

Grown fat and flabby on the pleasures of conquest Rome in its decadent years was susceptible to all manner of foreign religions. The introduction of the cult of Isis, of Serapis from Alexandria, and a variety of Great Mother salvation cults, were ample evidence that the official religion of the empire lacked the sense of mystery and closeness to the soil that the common people needed. It was not enough that the schools of philosophy had their rational systems; what the populace longed for was a religion with a heart. They sat doggedly through the offerings to the gods by the emperor and his family only to escape joyfully back to their own fertility festivals and local traditions. We have a picture of religion in the countryside – especially of the adoration of Pan as the Lord of Nature – in the Greek pastoral romance 'Daphnis and Chloe', written in the second century AD and attributed to Longus. This charming story tells of two infants discovered by shepherds and brought up by them to tend their sheep and goats. It combines an account of the innocent discovery of physical love with a portrait of the god Pan as miracle-worker with power over men's minds through his pipes.

This idyllic picture contrasts strongly with the works of Lucian, a Greek writer pre-dating Longus by some eighty years. Lucian's satirical sketches reflect a silly, corrupt society which he satirized with cynical levity. In his 'Auction of Philosophers', for example, Socrates, Aristotle and their colleagues are offered by the gods to the highest bidders. Where Longus offers escape from the turgid state religion and Lucian mocks it, Lucretius, writing in the first century BC, undermines it completely. In his philosophical poem 'On the Nature of Things' he tries to free man from his terror of the gods by advancing Epicurus's theory that the universe is made up of atoms; thus the course of the world could be explained without resorting to the idea of divine intervention.

cap, a tunic and a mantle on his left shoulder. Next to him stands the figure of a man with a lion's head mask, encircled by a serpent. This was Aion, the spirit of time and change.

The Mithras cult was very much 'officers and gentlemen only', including senior members of the civil administration. During the ceremonies, officials wore masks of cock's or

below The god Mithras slaying the great
bull from whose blood the created world
emerged. Note the serpent and the dog
devouring some of the holy blood,
symbolizing the darker aspects of human
nature. (Third century AD.)
left The Birth of Mithras. Mithras, bearing
a sword and torch to combat evil, emerging
from an egg. The egg is the symbol of
eternity. (Third century AD.)

left Magical hand from a Roman temple covered with symbols to avert the evil eye. The copulating figures in the wrist are surmounted by a ram's head representing Jupiter to whom offerings have been made for good fortune. A dualistic statement ends the design: the destructive cockatrice and the lustral pine cone used in Dionysiac ceremonies. (Second century AD.)

left Greek vase painting satirizing a Dionysian revel. The imitator of the god is carried by an ithyphallic clown, the maenad is a bony hag and the sacrificial bull becomes a donkey.

Throughout the body of Roman literature we see that the new godless philosophy made great breaches in the crumbling walls of the state religion; and as the intellectuals turned away from it, the people moved back to the old ecstatic and magical cults, absorbing the ancient beliefs of the country folk, as they returned to primitive worship.

Perhaps the best picture of the state of religion in the Roman world is contained in the only Latin novel that has come down to us in its entirety – *The Golden Ass* by Lucius Apuleius, a native of Madaura in Africa born around 114 AD. Apuleius borrowed heavily on his own wanderings for this comic, bawdy satire of life in second century Greece. In his picaresque story we learn of the current beliefs in magic and fate which he treats with the mocking irreverence of the confirmed cynic. Lucius's hero, being over-curious concerning the black arts, is accidentally turned into an ass by Photis, the beautiful servant of a witch, who recites the wrong charm. The intention was to turn Lucius into an eagle, but instead of sprouting wings he sprouted ears – a metamorphosis which enables the author to pour scorn on love-philtres and the like. (Apuleius himself was accused of using magic to win the hand of a wealthy widow. The accusations were made by the woman's brother-in-law from whom Apuleius stole her.)

Disguised as an ass, Lucius passes from master to master and sees, hears, and endures many strange things at the hands of robbers, eunuchs and magistrates. He is driven through a wealthy province where all around him he sees cheating, murder and the practice of the black arts whose punishment is death – a land steeped in corruption where the profession of soothsayer is a lucrative one though liable to end abruptly if prophecies do not come true.

The individual stories, though superficially gay and ironic – especially the delightful tale of Cupid and Psyche – are touched with the author's anxiety for a nation of people drifting rudderless on the seas of speculation and their dire need for spiritual guidance.

In one of his adventures as an ass Lucius falls into the hands of a group of priests of Cybele. The Romans called her the Great Mother and her cult, the fecundity of nature, was introduced into the Empire from Asia Minor. We have seen how near to the hearts of men the worship of the Earth Mother has been – a natural enough response by the primitive mind to the vagaries of nature. But in second-century Greece the cult had become corrupted and its priests were not above faking a miracle or two if it meant there were bribes to be extorted. And these miracles were effected with great good humour though spiced with

sufficient cruelty to make them attractive to depraved minds.

In this story Lucius describes the ecstatic dancing of the priests and their bizarre effeminate ways, how they dressed in women's clothes and jewellery – their faces painted with red ochre and flour and their hair crimped. This spectacle becomes the more horrific when we learn that they have castrated themselves in honour of the goddess of fertility!

It seems strange that this ecstatic craze involving castration and self-inflicted wounds should not only have swept through Greece, the home of rational philosophy, but also to have survived long enough to dance its frenzied way into Rome itself. On the face of it nothing could be more alien to the practical, disciplined Roman way of life than the Great Mother cult.

But we have evidence of this kind of self-mutilation from Roman statuary of the period. No doubt the sacrifice of the testicles would have seemed reasonable to the life-denying Stoic philosophers and it might not have appeared excessive to those who believed in the existence of the classical deities. The idea of offering the immediate source of life to the Great Mother would have seemed to the faithful an act of sublime beauty. But as the discriminating ass witnesses it for us, the whole business is merely an orgiastic method through which the priests dupe the masses to part with their goods and money under the guise of interceding with the gods on their behalf.

The sufferings of Lucius the ass have a direct bearing on the spiritual struggles of Apuleius, the thoughtful writer. In the ironic disguise of an ass, the author becomes a still point of sanity in a mad, corrupt world. Just as Paul the Apostle takes the Athenians to task for worshipping at the little shrine to the unknown god and proceeds to reason with them on the theme, so Lucius Apuleius, having depicted the extravagances, the fantasies and the cruelties of man, introduces his readers to the great goddess in the holy form of Isis. (Apuleius himself had been initiated into her mysteries.) He tells us of his vision on the sea shore at night, when all the stars of the heavens adorn the black robe of the goddess in whose silent beauty he finds fulfilment. In his adoration of Isis he senses that the goddess speaks to him and warns him to reform his way of life, that his past is forgiven and that now he can begin again. With the blessing of the goddess his symbolic asininity is removed, his human shape is restored and he returns to his normal life with a new awareness of the benign force of nature and her silent love of all mankind.

This religious concept was a blend of philosophy, an older Egyptian resurrection cult and the Roman idea of the

Great Mother, and as such was beyond the intellectual powers of the common herd of mankind. Yet Apuleius's book enjoyed a wide readership because of the humour of the writing and the very human story.

Two centuries after Apuleius, when Rome was in decline, the political and social unity of the Empire began to break up. Not only did the east and west split, but at one time three Caesars each claimed the Empire while ruling a part of it. The old Roman religion had become a formality and Christianity, once persecuted, was now openly practised. All over the Empire local deities were worshipped: in Britain the faithful made pilgrimages to springs where the Celtic goddesses lived who had healing powers; in Gaul the gods of hunting and the trees became important; in Italy the more esoteric fertility cults became secret societies and the country folk continued to stage ceremonies in the hopes of enlarging the harvest. The Germanic mercenaries who swept into the Empire, raiding and conquering, brought with them their own war god Tyr or Tiu (commemorated in our word 'Tuesday').

The pattern of family worship in the second and third centuries AD revolved around ancestor-worship and a fresh outbreak of old beliefs haphazardly accepted to fill the gap left by the empty formalism of the state religion. To thinking Romans the whole basis of their civilization must have appeared to be at stake. All around them they saw the revival of ancient, barbarous rituals with the state religion no longer the solid universal belief. Instead the religion of an oppressed minority was spreading throughout the Empire and it seemed likely to receive imperial patronage. More significantly, it was a religion which welcomed the common people. To the educated philosophers this new Christian cult would have been the very antithesis of religion as they knew it – the way to Truth and Beauty.

The Romans who worshipped the Olympian gods were bewildered by the new religious force of Christianity: they could not comprehend the idea of one God. Even the magic of the scriptures seemed alien to them. Reading of the Star of Bethlehem in the Gospel according to Matthew they argued that no star had ever led people to the same place, nor had it ever hovered over one spot. Although the astrologers amongst them were able to predict wonders, and the groupings of the stars were known to their philoso-phers, the behaviour of the Star of Bethlehem was beyond their credence.

As Christianity began to take root in the exhausted soil of the Empire, sorcerers and magicians saw in it a threat to their own influence. Simon Magus, a magician from Samaria, challenged the Apostles Peter and Paul, and to prove his own powers promised to fly up to heaven. He succeeded in levitating himself high into the air but after the Apostles' prayers he was cast down to earth again by the evil spirits which had enabled him to rise. (Simon then tried to purchase the Apostles' miraculous powers, hence our word 'simony'.)

The miracles surrounding the new religion – Paul's conversion, the healing of the sick, the Gift of Tongues, et cetera – appealed to the masses as very potent magic indeed, differing only in degree from the wonders worked in the ecstatic religions of classical legend.

Even so, it was a difficult task for Christians to com-pletely erase the old pagan beliefs and practices from among their converts. The magical squares of Pythagoras kept turning up hanging next to the cross on bracelets and necklaces, as did the triangular cabbalistic charm Abra-cadabra (said to be made up of the initials of the Hebrew word *Ab* (Father), *Ben* (Son), and *Ruach Acadsch* (Holy Spirit). Both these charms were used to protect the wearer against illness and misfortune and were evidence of a continuing need by the common people for magic as well

Chapter Three
Ritual AND*Terror*

as dogma. So enduring were the Pythagorean and Platonic concepts that an emergent religion, Gnosticism, tried to accommodate them to Christ-ian doctrine, teaching that knowledge and not belief was the key to salvation. Essentially mystic in character, some sects of Gnosticism introduced the ideas of non-Christian Greek and Oriental philosophers.

The heretical ideas of the Gnostics sparked off centuries of acrimonious debate within the Church and the great controversy has been preserved in the writings of the Church Fathers. In many ways Gnosticism was an attempt to explain Christian mysteries in terms of magic derived from classical philosophy. Though the different groups varied greatly in their teachings, they usually agreed that the world was brought into being not by God but by a 'Demi-urge' – a being subordinate to the Supreme Being and sometimes conceived as the author of evil. Between God and the Demi-urge were a num-ber of powerful spirit-beings known as Archons. It was an Archon who was sent by God to redeem the world in the shape of Jesus Christ. Christ, according to the Gnostics, was a subordinate power to God, a divine attribute personified, like Mind, Truth or Logos. Since some sections of Gnostic belief were carefully worked out as a philosophical system, it had an immediate appeal to the educated classes: Gnosis or 'special knowledge', assured them that only they – the initiated – would be saved on the Day of Judgment.

Gnosticism flourished in second-century Rome at a time when the Empire was still the greatest power in the world. Its ideas were developing in parallel with Christian pre-cepts; but in Egypt Gnostic groups absorbed other magical elements such as the worship of the child Horus who was invoked for protection against evil. The faithful carried small images of the Gnostic Horus (who was depicted as a boy with his finger on his lips) to ward off crocodiles and robbers and to assure the soul a safe passage to the other world where it would be watched over by the parents of Horus, Isis and Osiris.

Gnosticism was not a homogeneous religion; each group worshipped as an entity in itself and the very separation of these groups symbolized the political divisions amongst the provinces of the Roman Empire, especially in North Africa. The quarrels of the different groups as they pamphleteered

left The Adoration of the Magi, a fifteenth-century triptych. The Wise Men's gifts symbolize the attributes of Christ as the King and Lord: gold for kingship, frankincense for divinity and myrrh for suffering and death.

against each other's heresies foreshadowed a more significant upheaval – the break-up of Roman Africa.

The great city of Alexandria, as the pivot of Africa, the meeting place of Greek and Egyptian, Arab and Jew, of Levantine and Roman, was a natural hotbed of dissension. Its library, perhaps the eighth wonder of the ancient world, was the international centre of learning which combined with its museum contained all the accumulated knowledge of the classical world. At Alexandria philosophers and poets taught and disputed; healers and prophets practised their callings in the market place. Christian argued with Christian while sun-worshippers recruited followers, and sorcerers sold magic philtres.

The study and practice of Alchemy, as the derivation of the Arabic word suggests (*al-kimia* – the art of the Egyptians) developed in Alexandria. It originated from a very ancient belief that the black mud of the Nile floods had magical properties of creating life. In Ptolemaic times amalagam was used in a primitive metal-plating process. One of the great exponents of Alchemy was an Alexandrian Jewess, Maria Prophetissa, who invented a glass vessel with two spouts at differing heights on the neck for separating chemicals during distillation.

Charles Kingsley gives us a vivid portrait of fifth-century Alexandria as a crowded, turbulent city in his historical novel *Hypatia*. Hypatia was the beautiful daughter of the mathematician, Theon. Her teaching of Neoplatonic philosophy so enraged the fanatical Alexandrian monks that they incited a Christian mob to tear her limb from limb. Jews were also the target of such attacks – especially the rich merchants who lived by the harbour – because they, among all the welter of religious beliefs, clung to their faith in the one and only God, the Creator of Heaven and Earth. Such obduracy infuriated Christian as well as pagan sensibilities because it was a unitarian rather than a trinitarian belief.

A century before Hypatia Alexandria achieved a special notoriety as the home of the priest Arius the Heresiarch. Arius and his followers reasoned that as Jesus had been born only a couple of centuries before their time he could not be the equal of God the Father in the Trinity. This heresy led to such a virulent dispute amongst Christian bishops that in 325 the Emperor Constantine was forced to convene the Council of Nicaea in Bithynia, Asia Minor, to pronounce on the problem once and for all. At this first ecumenical council the Arian heresy was condemned and the bishops agreed in one accord that Christ was the Son of the Father before the earth was created.

Throughout Europe at this time and particularly in Eastern Germany and Poland there was great tribal unrest. People were on the move, either driven out of their homes by marauding bands down the Saxon and Baltic shores or

left The fall of Simon Magus. The great magician is cast down to earth by St Peter from the height of his levitation.

above Reproductions of engraved gems with Gnostic symbols and charms. (Second to fourth century AD.)

above left The mermaid Melusina carrying her cup of temptation and her mirror. The mirror symbolizes the moon, ruler of the tides. She was a direct descendant of the water-sprites of antiquity. Thirteenth-century woodcarving from Ireland.

left A medieval concept of a nature spirit depicted as an old woman with the body of a sea-horse. On a thirteenth-century choir stall, Southall Minster, England.

below Punic stela from Carthage. This
funerary monument shows the gods of
Carthage above the pediment of a temple.
At the top the Sun and Moon, above the
fertility goddess Tanit (Astarte) and below,
the Cartheginian equivalents of Dionysus,
Cupid and Venus.

leaving to enlist in the Roman armies. The warlike Goths, a Swedish tribe, had set out on a career of conquest and by 269 they had entrenched themselves along the Danube. About the year 340 the whole tribe were converted to Christianity by Bishop Wulfila – to the Arian version of the religion. (It is arguable that their old religion based on Wotan as the father of the gods made the Arian doctrine more acceptable to them than the orthodox Christian tenet.) The mass conversion of the Goths was something of a victory for the Arians since the tribe held most of Eastern Europe under the threat of war.

But in 363 the Huns swept into the Danube basin, conquering the Goths who either submitted to their new masters or became refugees, wandering south. The history of the Goths is important since in the course of being dispersed around the Empire they suddenly turned upon Rome at the beginning of the fifth century. The legions were hastily summoned home from the outposts of the Empire to defend the capital, but in 410 the Visigothic war-chief Alaric captured the city and sacked it in three terrible days of pillage and rape.

In the wake of the Goths came another Baltic group, the Ostrogoths, who fought their way across Europe under their leader Theodoric. After a three-year campaign against Roman armies Theodoric became ruler of all Italy. Like his people he believed in Arianism but he kept his tribe united and established friendly relations with the Romans. Theodoric died in 526, and after a series of wars his kingdom fell under the Catholic mantle of the Byzantine Emperor Justinian. But the sword could not entirely eradicate the heretical cult of Arius; although Arianism had been repudiated by Catholics within the Empire there were still pockets in southern France and the Iberian Peninsula where the Ostrogoths remained powerful and nurtured their religion much to the chagrin of orthodox Christians. These religious differences hardened into mutually exclusive doctrines and became a source of future religious controversy.

Religious theory and dogma were the province of the educated churchman, but where did the common man fit into these dialectical struggles? In Britain, at least, Celtic Christians enjoyed a certain autonomy in the practice of their religion – even to the point of arguing with Augustine of Canterbury over the proper date for Easter. Yet the rituals of pre-Christian culture survived. King Arthur is said to have carried a painting of the Virgin Mary on his shield yet the wishing wells and temples of the old water sprites were frequented long after the time of the Saxon

above Two scenes from Roman Alexandria taken from Charles Kingsley's novel 'Hypathia'.
upper The secrecy of Christians in the time of persecution.
lower Religious turmoil in the city: a monk fights with an Arab.

above The jewelled crown of the Visigothic kings of Spain. (Sixth century AD.) **left** The tomb of Theodoric the Ostrogoth at Ravenna. The Arian king tolerated the Catholic beliefs of the Roman people though he maintained the religious precepts of his own people.

conquest. This same confusion of the sacred and the profane and the sniping of religious factions at one another was a feature of life well into the seventh century.

(Around this time, too, in Visigothic Spain the first Black Mass was performed. In theory a Requiem Mass is said for the souls of the dead. Some magician cunningly reasoned that the obverse must be viable too: if a Requiem Mass were said for a *living* person their soul might leave the body and the subject would die. Even today the black wax candles used for a Requiem are blasphemously employed by some magical sects to celebrate Black Mass.)

While the Latin peoples in southern Europe wrangled over their religious differences there were stirrings among the northern tribes – the Saxons, Angles, Danes, and Jutes. When the great warrior Atilla, King of the Huns, swept through the eastern Empire he appeared like the apocalypse, filling Christian hearts with dread. They called him 'The Scourge of God', and they saw his rampaging horsemen as a punishment visited on Rome for the evils it had committed in the world. Atilla himself adopted the title as a convenient piece of propaganda to cow the more recalcitrant of his enemies. Christendom believed the fiction because of the guilt they felt over the theological divisions within their ranks. But for all their acknowledged culpability it was the heathen tribes to the north who bore the brunt of the Hun invasion.

The great push from the east by Atilla's armies in the middle of the fifth century, coupled with the crumbling social and religious fabric of the tribes within the Empire, created a groundswell which led to mass migrations. Tribes like the Angles and the Saxons uprooted themselves and took their wives and cattle across the North Sea in flat-bottomed boats to settle in Britain. Instead of their usual summer sorties for plunder, these pirate-farmers emigrated permanently to rich new pastures and oak forests teeming with deer and wild boar.

The invading Saxons brought to Britain their metalwork crafts, some rather poor pottery, their enduring dislike of towns (as a farming people they lived mainly in loose-knit villages) and a quantity of exotic legends. Their greatest surviving poem relates the deeds of Beowulf the Scilding. It tells of the Hall of the King which is terrorized by a monster called Grendel. This mystical, half-human beast carries off thanes of the king by night and tears them apart before diving to his lair under a haunted lake where his mother, a water-hag, lives. Beowulf traps Grendel in the Hall and in the ensuing battle he mortally wounds the monster. Grendel's mother comes the next night to avenge

her son's death. Beowulf plunges into the lake after her and slays her with a magic sword. In time Beowulf becomes king and fifty years later he meets his death while in combat with a fire-breathing dragon who guards an immense treasure. In this romantic tale we hear little of gods but much of magic and potent charms.

From folk poetry and legend of the time we know that the Saxon settlers in Britain transported their gods with them. They build temples of timber to worship Wotan, Thunar and the Spring Maiden. The head of the house led the family in worship and the womenfolk knew of magic charms and herbs for curing the sick. In these pursuits the new immigrants differed very little from their Celtic neighbours, except that the newcomers were heathen while the Celts were now Christian.

The Saxon take-over of Britain was a slow process. Beginning on the Sussex and Kentish coasts it gradually moved further inland, generation by generation, as families required more farming land for their sons. The pirate-farmers became warrior-farmers as they struck north to gain more territory in the name of their god Wotan, in whose honour they drank horsebroth on ceremonial occasions.

To Saxon sensibilities Christianity must have seemed an extraordinary cult: the idea of a gentle Jesus and the practice of loving one's enemies were foreign to their way of thinking. Alien too were the monks who wore black and lived in isolated communities. But when Augustine, a missionary from Rome, baptized King Ethelbert in 597, Saxon England became Christian. Again the Saxons were awestruck when Augustine dared to build a shrine to his gentle Jesus right beside the great Celtic god of Creation, Cernunnos. An action calculated to demand at least religious equality for Christianity!

But Christianity took an early hold on Saxon England. The Venerable Bede refers in his writings to the practical missionary work of Bishop Wilfrid of Northumbria in the seventh century who, during a terrible drought, taught the farmers of Sussex, where he lived in exile, the art of net-making and sea-fishing. Here was a Christian who gave the Saxons practical knowledge for self-preservation – something that their own medicine men and gods had not done. As an exercise in Christian public relations this did more to win the hearts and minds of these superstitious southerners to the new religion than all the preachings of the monastic orders.

Yet for all their dedication to the new religion the more ancient pagan ceremonies continued, and many of these have survived down to our own times: the May Day dances

left The god Odin shown with his two ravens (representing thought) and two wolves (the past and the future) as the master of all knowledge. Nineteenth-century, by Bertel Thorwaldsen.
below A fifteenth-century reconstruction of Odin depicted as the wielder of lightning. He rides his eight-legged horse Sleipnir.

with green boughs derive from the Celtic Maypole dance, a celebration of the symbolic penis of Cernunnos, creator of life and wisdom, and 'Lord of the Centre'. In these celebrations village virgins vied with one another for the honour of being chosen as the Spring Maiden, Godgifu, the gift of god. The girl most deserving of respect rode naked on horseback through the village accompanied by dancing maidens in a symbolic procession to welcome in the Spring.

Saxon thanes were content to turn their heathen temples into churches which generally meant replacing pagan images and charms with crosses. And if they were no longer allowed to drink horsebroth in honour of Wotan and were obliged to learn new prayers, they soon confused these with

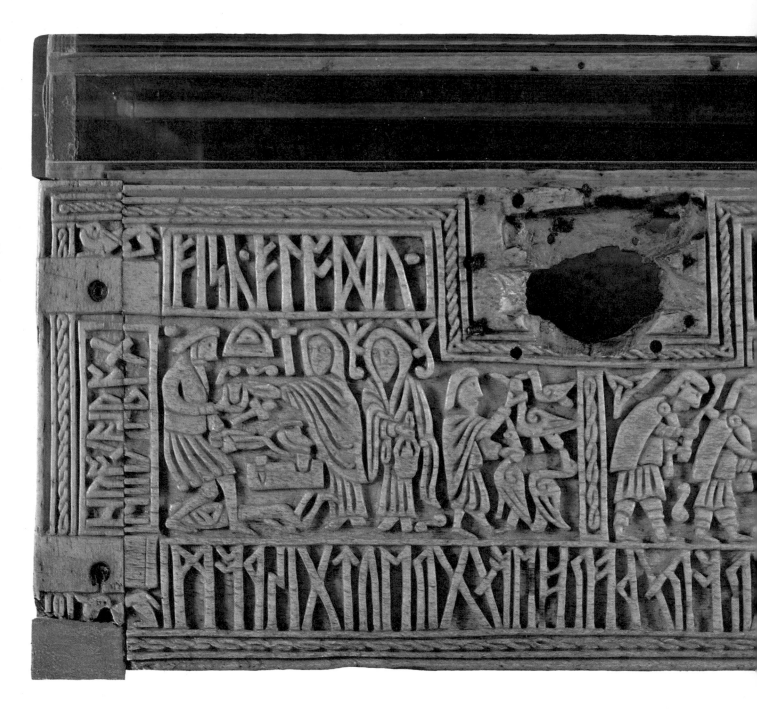

the older chants and maintained the spirit if not the outward form of the deep-rooted ancient beliefs. But they appear to have been no less Christian for all that.

At about the same time in the east, the Prophet Mohammed had united the peoples of Arabia in a new unitarian faith and under the banner of Islam his armies swept into Europe. So deep was the faith of an Arab commander under the Caliph Omar that in 642 he ordered Alexandria's thousand-year-old library to be burnt when his Muslims captured the city. He reasoned that one word revealed by God through the Holy Koran was worth all the accumulated writings of infidels. The ashes of the most important library of the ancient world blew across the desert for months. In spite of this act of vandalism the conquering armies of Islam laid the foundations for a civilization of great beauty and intellectual achievement in the conquered territories of Roman North Africa.

below The Franks Casket: front panel of
an eighth-century Anglo-Saxon jewel box.
On the right are shown the Magi bringing
gifts to the Christ child. On the left the
heathen legend of Weland the Smith.
Captured and cruelly lamed by the Swedish
king Nidudr, Weland avenges himself by
murdering the king's sons and presenting their
gold-set and bejewelled remains to the family.

so much the better!

Haroun er Raschid was a contemporary of the Frankish Emperor Charlemagne and he sent the founder of the Holy Roman Empire a gift of a water clock with artificial singing birds. This curiosity became part of the folklore of European magic and is linked in the same tradition to the accusations against Bishop Gerber some two hundred years later of owning a talking head.

But in spite of such imperial gifts between powerful rulers, east and west were divided both politically and religiously. In the ninth century, as in previous times, the peasants still clung to their ritual observance of the seasons and kept in close contact with nature. And in Islam a sect of Mohammedan ascetic mystics formalized a general belief among them that a man's inner being could establish contact with the spiritual world into the doctrine of the Sūfi. This sect with its deliberately paradoxical and contradictory writings designed to open the minds of its initiates was to become deeply influential to future occultists.

Every army of occupation is susceptible to local customs and the Mohammedan soldiers began to assimilate the secret and ancient magical practices of the Berber tribes of Morocco. Up until the early part of this century the Berbers practised a secret religion under the guidance of priestesses.

The Berbers joined the banner of Islam and crossed the Mediterranean under the leadership of Tariq, an Arab who in 710 defeated Roderick the Gothic King of Spain – a nation which had become weak and corrupt. The modern name of the site of this victory is Gibraltar, being a corruption of Gebel-al-Tariq, the hill of Tariq.

As Tariq's Moslem forces pressed north the fleeing Goths settled in Galicia, in northern Spain, and they watched the conquering armies prepare their invasion of France. But the Paladins of Charlemagne defeated the armies of Islam and contained them south of the Pyrenees where they began to spread their faith and sow the seeds of their folk customs. These fell on fertile ground as far as the populace of the ancient Roman province were concerned.

Perhaps one of the most noteworthy aspects of the Islamic civilization was their tolerance and, indeed, protection of the Jewish communities in their midst – an enlightened attitude which later produced one of the greatest thinkers of medieval times, the philosopher Maimonides. Equally important, it allowed the growth of a reaction to Maimonides's philosophy, a reaction which generated the Kabbala movement with its mystical interpretation of the Scripture.

Apart from the Holy teachings of the Koran the Arabs also brought with them their beliefs in magic as expressed in the famous tales of the Arabian Nights. The source of the tales told of Haroun er Raschid, Caliph of Bagdad, is obscure; some were Persian, some ancient Egyptian, but they illustrate the kind of magical phenomena that exercised the imaginations of the ordinary people in the Islamic world – flying horses, ghosts, genies, angels and enchanters. And if they were relished equally by the wise and learned

In the eighth and ninth centuries Islam had reached the zenith of its power. The Caliph in Baghdad was regarded as the earthly representative of the Prophet and both the spiritual and political leader of the Faithful. The title in Arabic meant 'successor' – the successor of Mohammed – and as such he was regarded as something more than human. In 723 the Caliph decreed that within his dominions all images should be removed from Christian churches. His Muslim subjects believed that to reproduce men and animals in paint or stone was an insult to God the Creator. The Christians, it seems, were in a frame of mind to accept this decree. In the neighbouring Byzantine empire Leo III followed the Caliph's lead by pronouncing against the use of icons in Byzantine churches, a law which was made absolute in 730 and continued in force until 843.

This ban created further tension with Rome as Pope Gregory IV took exception to Leo III's high-handed action in making a religious law without papal concurrence. Matters worsened when the Emperor wrested from Rome the religious jurisdiction over his southern Italian provinces.

above left A whirling Dervish from Central Turkey. The ever-increasing tempo of his dance induced ecstasy, culminating hopefully in a union with the Divine. Early nineteenth century.

left A magician's robe from the northern borders of the Sahara. The diagrams and geometric patterns have a magical meaning to the initiated. The Arabic text comes from the Koran. Mid-nineteenth century.

right A film reconstruction of a Czech-Jewish legend. In the thirteenth century Rabbi Loew is said to have made a humanoid monster, the Golem, to be his servant. A young man discovered the magic words to activate the Golem. He was unable to control it and after killing him the Golem marched away destroying anything in its path.

The stage was set for the great schism. Already both sides were accusing each other of heresy and of serving Satanic ends. In 1054 the Eastern Orthodox Church based in Byzantium rejected the claims of the Popes in Rome to be the supreme rulers of the Church on earth. The reasons for the split were tragically political; by then the west had been torn apart by further wars and the incursion of the Danes and the Viking raids from the north.

We have to look at the social structure of life in ninth-century Norway to understand this gradual insurgence of heathen tribes into western Europe. The Kings of Norway began to pressure the free land-holders into paying taxes and claimed the right to oversee inheritances. This was anathema to the Norse farmers who had never submitted to kings and who had amassed tidy nest-eggs for themselves by the practice of Sumer-lading, that is by spending the summer raiding along the French and English coasts.

These heathen warrior-farmers worshipped Odin Grey-beard and Thor Redbeard and they carried with them a number of magical charms always including a miniature hammer of Thor and the magical runes, characters of the earliest Teutonic alphabet, which were given to mankind by the gods for writing prayers and charms.

Although the Viking raids were at first only on a small scale, they were terrible and savage in the havoc they wrought on the Saxon farmers. The red beard of Thor could be seen flaming over gutted abbeys where his hammer had been thrown by his followers. These Norse-men were superstitious and they responded violently to the sight of processions of singing monks carrying the cross of Christ as if they were warlocks casting spells. They would cut the monks to pieces and lay waste the towns and villages in the area.

The Norse noblemen were quick to realize that there were profits to be made from these raids and territorial expansion into the bargain, so they began to organize larger expeditions. Armies led by kings pushed their black and gold longships off the Scandinavian coast and set out across the North Sea to plunder and conquer new lands.

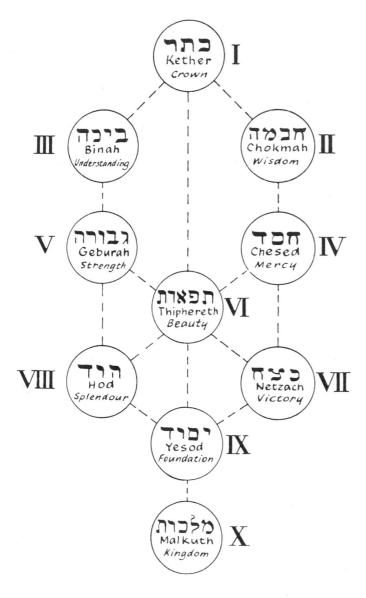

The diagram shows the Tree of Sephiroth with the following positions:

כתר
Kether
Crown — I

בינה
Binah
Understanding — III

חכמה
Chokmah
Wisdom — II

גבורה
Geburah
Strength — V

חסד
Chesed
Mercy — IV

תפארת
Thiphereth
Beauty — VI

הוד
Hod
Splendour — VIII

נצח
Netzach
Victory — VII

יסוד
Yesod
Foundation — IX

מלכות
Malkuth
Kingdom — X

above right A magic mirror for divination. Made from oak, pewter and black glass according to Kabbalistic precepts. (Eighteenth century.)

above The Tree of Sephiroth. This diagram which is central to all Kabbalistic magic shows the inter-relationship between the Divine attributes in the work of Creation.

right Anglo-Saxon cross of the eighth century in the churchyard at Carew, Pembrokeshire, Wales. The carvings on the transept are Christian; the lower ones are derived from the heathen myth of Sigurd the Volsung.

right inset Irish High Cross of the ninth century from Castle Dermot, Co. Kildare, Ireland. The decorative panels reflect a fusion of Irish Celtic and Nordic designs.

But the spirit of Christianity, in the shape of missionaries, had begun to reach the north. The northern kings astutely realized the political benefits of adopting the religion of the more civilized south. Olaf Trygvasson, King of Norway between 995 and 1000, invaded England with Sweyn of Denmark and attacked London in 994. He harried the coast from Northumberland to Scilly where, according to the Heimskringla – the history of the Norse kings – he was converted to Christianity. On his return the next year to Norway he deposed Haakon the Bad and forcibly imposed the new religion on his subjects.

Evidence of the cross-fertilization of the two religions can still be seen in England: notably in the ivory Franks casket in the British Museum and in the many Northumbrian stone crosses to be found in English churchyards, on which heathen gods are depicted side by side with Christian saints and symbols.

In those war-torn years leading up to the first millenium, western Europe ran with blood. The monks who chronicled the times interpreted the march of armies as divine vengeance visited on a sinful humanity. In Norway it is recorded that villagers saw strange signs in the sky and great balls of coloured fire swooping overhead. To the heathen mind such symbols would have heralded the Ragnarok (Twilight of the Gods), unleashing Fenris the Wolf of Doom, whose gaping jaws could touch earth and heaven. The apocalyptic wolf would be at large in the land to devour the gods and mankind. But these recent converts to Christianity saw the marvels as the approach of the year 1000 – the millenium which might well bring with it the Day of Judgment.

It was hardly surprising that Christian and heathen alike predicted the imminent end of humanity in some terrible cataclysmic event. The greatest power in the world, Islam, had lost its unity: a separate Caliphate had been set up in Spain while in North Africa several Arab kings squabbled amongst themselves. The seas were full of pirates, Norse and Arab; the churches of east and west were locked in a bitter quarrel over the supremacy of the Bishop of Rome; and life was rendered even more precarious by the plagues that swept the world like a divine curse.

As war, plague and religious controversy blew over two continents, the common people of the western world went about their work, tilling the fields, tending the cattle, and eking out a living from the land as best they could. They were subject to military service under their Master's banner and were liable to be called upon by the monks to prepare ground for building churches or help cultivate church

lands. If their simple faith in Christianity kept them bound to the Church it was less the teachings of monks that ensured their devotion than the ancient practices shrewdly countenanced by the Popes, albeit reluctantly. Every village had its wise woman who knew all about herbs, its horse whisperer who could cure a sick horse just by reciting magic incantations into its ear, and of course, there were the four seasonal festivals of the farmer's year.

Throughout Europe the year ended on November 2nd, All Souls Day, when prayers and alms were offered to alleviate the suffering of souls in purgatory (a holy day instituted in 993 by the Abbot of Cluny). On this day farmers would put cattle into the byre or slaughter the unwanted ones. At Christmas the great religious feast took place which was followed by fire ceremonies to encourage the return of the sun. At the Feast of Purification people celebrated the first snowdrops; at Easter they gave eggs – a life symbol – and chased after Easter hares whose leaping movements had sexual connotations. In England on May Day there were the maypoles, the naked Godivas, and the exchange of gifts, such as love-knots intertwined with flowers. (The German pretzel derives from this custom. In some Swabian villages today young men pin a pretzel to the door of their beloved.) On Midsummer Eve young men and women jumped over bonfires hand in hand to gain the blessing of the magic night. In August The Mummers' Play would be performed when the horned masks would be brought out and the wounding of the midsummer sun enacted. Another Mummer's play centres around St George who is killed in a duel only to be brought to life, symbolizing the death of the year and its resurrection in the spring. The cycle of the year was completed with the fruit festivals of early September and eventually the All Souls celebration once again.

So it can be seen that the tedium of life was punctuated with enough feast days and celebrations to keep the peasantry in a state of cheerful quiescence – all their aggressions being channelled into riotous ceremonies and traditional observances.

But some were not satisfied by the boisterous public celebration of the seasons. For King Edgar to proclaim in 959 'that every priest zealously promote Christianity, and totally extinguish every heathenism; and forbid wellworshippings, and necromancies, and divinations and enchantments' showed that there were groups of people who kept themselves apart and performed secret rites: their dances could not be tolerated by the Church and they were thought of as witches.

above Anglo-Saxon charm for catching a swarm of bees, written in the margin of a manuscript.

49

Contrary to popular prediction the world did not end in the year 1000. But the year was a watershed in that during the following century the political order in England became stabilized under the strong central government of kings like William the Conqueror. The feudal system introduced by William into England provided a social fabric which was to last until the Industrial Revolution. In western Europe Mother Church was a power unto itself and the clergy vied with monarchs for influence and wealth. In the east Byzantium continued to rule a highly civilized and rich state, and to the south the Islamic kingdoms of North Africa maintained a great intellectual tradition in their renowned religious schools from Central Asia to Spain.

As the political and religious order of western Europe hardened, the fear of heathenism receded and, with the fear, the laws against it. Witchcraft, hitherto regarded as heathenism, was now classed with sorcery and poisoning under laws passed by William I. This new enlightenment may have had something to do with the unceremonious attitude of the king himself. An astrologer sailed with William's Norman armies to invade England, but met his death on the way across when his boat was sunk, one of two which were lost. William joked that if the man could not even predict the weather then his demise was no great tragedy. It is more surprising to find a magician accompanying an army that fought under banners blessed by the Pope.

Again in 1070, when William had to lead his men into the marshy ground of the fen country to put down a rebellion by Hereward the Wake at Ely, he picked up an old woman at Brandon in Norfolk who was said to be a witch. Her part in the war effort was to stand in a wooden tower and hurl curses at the Saxons. She appeared to have less effect on them than on William for in a raid they burnt down the tower and the poor woman perished in the flames. Such incidents remind us that for all the realities of power men still believed that they needed God *and* the magicians on their side.

There was a story current that William I was descended from the Devil (as well as being the son of a tradesmen's daughter!) It is not unexpected then that his son William Rufus was also suspected of demonic origin. A fit of ungovernable temper was sufficient evidence of the cloven hoof. Like most of the ruling families in Europe at the time

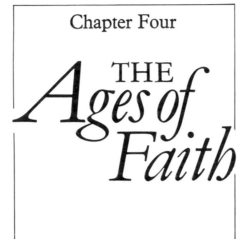

Chapter Four
THE *Ages of Faith*

William I's ancestors had been heathen only a century earlier. Though cowering clerks and scribes might deduce William Rufus's diabolic birth from his violent rages it is quite probable that the family themselves traced their lineage back to Odin Greybeard.

The mysterious circumstances surrounding the death of William Rufus gave rise to the theory that this unscrupulous man had been sacrificed to the old Celtic gods. G. M. Trevelyan describes him as 'not without kingly qualities . . . [but] a ruffian only pious when on his sick bed'. His greed for revenue and his abuse of his lay vassals brought him into direct conflict with the Church. When Lanfranc, his father's Archbishop, died William refused to appoint a successor and for five years he kept the see of Canterbury vacant and collected its revenue himself. When he was taken ill and thought to be dying he appointed the reluctant Anselm as Archbishop. 'Then, to the surprise and grief of his subjects he recovered, and for years led the saintly Archbishop such a life as fully explains the comic and almost cowardly reluctance that Anselm had shown to accept the post. . . .' William Rufus died in a hunting accident; apparently he had been mistaken for a stag. But the significance of the date of the accident should not be overlooked: 2 August 1100, the date of one of the great festivals honouring the Celtic Lord of the Woods, Cernunnos, the horned god to whom humans had been sacrificed in ancient times.

Kings and rulers had always been a fertile source of popular superstition and this phenomenon reached its height in the eleventh and twelfth centuries. In the east both the Byzantine emperor and the Caliph of Islam were regarded by the faithful as men blessed with the right to rule in order to protect the true religion. In the west kingship evolved from the function of the old tribal chiefs whose divinity was linked to the fertility gods. Thus the link between the king and the fortunes of the soil was basic to the idea of feudalism, a system that gave paramount importance to the king as its head. If the king was weak or feeble the crops would reflect his constitution; if strong and vigorous, the crops would be plentiful.

When the Christian Church imposed its own traditions over the old heathenism it stated unequivocally that the king was the anointed of God – an idea taken directly from

above The Holy Roman Emperor
Frederick II whose diplomatic contacts with
Mohammedan leaders laid him open to the
charge of heresy.
right The defeated rebel Hereward the
Wake pays homage to William I of England.
In the campaign against Hereward, William
had employed the services of the Witch of
Brandon.

left The slaying of William II (Rufus) of England by Sir Walter Tyrrell in the New Forest. The circumstances surrounding the 'accident' suggest that it might have been a ritual sacrifice.
below An English silver coin (known as a touch-piece) for healing the 'King's Evil', from the reign of George III, depicting St George Slaying the Dragon.

the biblical account of the choice of Saul and David. The notion that the touch of the king could cure scrofula (the 'King's Evil') prevailed from the reign of Edward the Confessor.

The uncontrollable rages of kings and their resultant unchristian behaviour easily laid them open to the accusation that they were driven by demons – not only to the destruction of their own immortal soul but to that of their countries as well. The Church might excommunicate the man or place his lands under an interdict, but this was seen for what it was – a purely political move of little temporal effect. Certainly the brilliant and unruly Frederick II, ruler of the Holy Roman Empire (1220–50) took little heed when he was excommunicated by Pope Gregory IX. Frederick, the grandson of Barbarossa, belonged to the supposedly demon-fathered line of Hohenstaufen emperors from southern Germany where their beautiful mountain castle still survives. A skilful soldier and resourceful statesman, Frederick's ambition was to create an empire larger than Charlemagne's and to this end he tried to integrate Italy and Sicily into a single united kingdom within his empire. This brought him into armed conflict with Popes Gregory IX and Innocent IV.

Frederick was one of the most cultured men of his age whose interests extended to mathematics, natural history, medicine and other branches of intellectual activity, but his open declaration of his disbelief in the teachings of the Church brought down accusations of 'Antichrist' on his head – an inevitable conclusion in the contemporary European mind when his political achievements were accomplished in spite of the papal interdict. Furthermore Frederick's tolerance of Mohammedans in his service led the papal party to accuse him of being the author of the blasphemous (and imaginary) work, *De Tribus Impostoribus* – Moses, Jesus and Mohammed, all accused of being imposters!

One of Frederick's most impressive achievements was the success of the Fifth Crusade in 1228. By simple diplomatic agreements with Arab leaders he avoided the usual carnage and negotiated unrestricted access for pilgrims to the holy places of Christendom. In the following year he was crowned King of Jerusalem. For him the blood-stained black comedy of the crusades was over; but to the western Christian mind even to sit down across a table with Mohammedans was trafficking with the devil. Frederick must be demonically inspired, churchmen reasoned, if he can hobnob with heathens, defy the Pope's temporal power and lead a thoroughly licentious and self-indulgent life

Matthew Rossell. Inu.

upper left The miraculous power of holy relics. A murdered man, thrown into the tomb of the Prophet Elisha, immediately returns to life. An eighteenth-century engraving.

lower left A blind lady of Bologna has her sight restored after intercession to Our Lady of the Annunciation. A seventeenth-century engraving.

left St Christopher carrying the Christ child across a treacherous river (the river of death) — an act which enshrined him as the protector of all travellers. Engraving by Albrecht Dürer, 1511.

above The blind St Cecilia, patron Saint of the blind and of musicians. This third-century Roman martyr is said to have invented the organ.

above St Sebastian, the Patron Saint of
archers, pin-makers and of soldiers,
depicted here with angels as his train
bearers.
below Demonic assignation: a witch-wife
and her Demon lover. Woodcut by Ulrich
Molitor, 1489.

without meeting his just rewards. Naturally it meant that
he had to find his friends only among heretics and magicians,
since it was more than worth a Christian's soul to be in his
company.

So much for kings and popes. What of the common
people at the beginning of the Middle Ages? What of their
festivals, their May Day dances, fire-leaping at midsummer,
and their ignorance? Their life depended on the rotation
of the crops and careful husbandry. The epicentre of this
annual round of planting, growing and harvesting was the
village church, more often than not sited upon some
ancient holy place whose god had become the church's
saint. The Church taught that this god-cum-saint would
look after their affairs in heaven, and so to their delight
the peasants began to find their magic in the Church.

The uneducated masses had no sense of history. They
were unaware of the distant past and knew only what they
heard from the pulpit, local gossip and the tales handed
down from their fathers. All their efforts were directed
towards observing the proper festivals which would bring
help from the saints to keep the year turning, as well as
offering a release from the drudgery of the land in the
enjoyment of feasts and fairs. The priest of Inverkeithing
was punished in the twelfth century for leading the girls
of his parish in a dance around an ancient stone phallus;
but every village had its maypole, and around it the most
modest of maidens tripped on May Day with garlands in
their hair.

Within the Church itself were there not many magical
blessings to be won by making a pilgrimage to the shrine
of some specially powerful saint, like Thomas à Becket of
Canterbury? Men had heard that these pilgrimages were
sometimes the scene of miraculous cures – and if the cures
were not real at least they brought peace to the troubled
heart. It was said that to step into the holy well at Walsing-
ham in Norfolk was to join the Virgin Mary in ecstatic
communion, and to witness the gifts and offerings from
royal pilgrims in the priory church was a sight of surpassing
wonder. In hundreds of churches throughout Europe there
were holy relics, bones and pieces of hair of the saints, and
enough fragments of the Holy Cross to recreate a forest on
Calvary. Each of these relics was believed by the simple,
uncritical worshippers to contain enormous power.

While the theologians in their seminaries engaged in
rarefied debate as to how many angels could stand on the
point of a needle, the mass of the people were ignorant of
the Church hierarchy and the bishops who ruled it.
Though some great churchmen did stand out above their

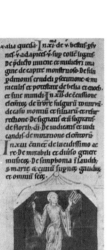

The ecstacy of St Hildegarde of Bingen. She carries a writing tablet and engraving tool. Her amanuensis **below** writes her description of the vision. **below right** St Dominic de Guzman presiding over the burning of Albigensian manuscripts. Fifteenth-century painting by P. Berreguete.

colleagues for their extraordinary scholarship or saintliness their names were unknown to the general congregation except as passing references in sermons. The humble church-goers learnt their catechism from the local priest and saw it illustrated in paintings on the church walls. But nobody explained to them why it was wrong to hang a hollow stone in the stable to keep malignant spirits away, nor were the women who nursed the sick warned not to confuse old magic chants with the psalms; the horse-whisperer still fidgeted through the sermon before hurrying off to mouth his incantations into the ear of an ailing mare.

At Easter when the people gave thanks for the resurrection of the Lord who could separate that event from the rebirth of the land and the sudden flowering of nature? And was it not diverting to do what one had seen one's grandmother do on such an occasion – to plant sticks decorated with blue and white ribbons around a lucky wishing well? If Whitsun brought the apple-blossom then what more appropriate celebration than that a pretty girl should ride naked through the village to prove the victory of Mother Nature over the dark powers of winter? Even the clergy entered into the annual rite of cleaning the giant chalk hill-carvings at Cerne Abbas and Wilmington, and by so doing they added their blessing to a time-honoured folk custom, one that was supposed to bring luck to the participants. So we see that Christianity and nature were inextricable in the minds of medieval serfs and it was more than the Church could do to unravel the threads.

Although some of the educated bishops had their doubts about the primitive aspects of saints' days and they instituted the occasional inquiry, for two centuries after the millennium there were very few prosecutions for heresy in England. There were, however, reports of strange happenings – cattle being cured or dropping dead or crops failing suddenly because of spells. (One method apparently was to harness a toad to a tiny model plough and set it loose in the field to kill the fertility of the soil.) But it seems that the clerical courts gave serious attention only to people of substance – either educated men who could persuade others by their writings or people of sufficient standing for their irregular activities to cause a public scandal.

In the wilder regions of England, particularly to the west in the foot-hills of the Welsh mountains (the home of the Celts), the ancient beliefs persisted in spite of the Church. The wishing well, the spirit who lives in the oak tree, fairies and ogres were as real to them still as the saints of the Catholic Church.

In Europe around the beginning of the eleventh century a new religious cult of holiness was making its presence felt, extending its influence over southern Germany, Italy and southern France. The Bogomili were a heretical sect which eventually broke away from the Greek Church. They were called after a Bulgarian monk, a reformer of the tenth century. Their founder, Basilius, was burnt by the Byzantine emperor, Alexius Comnenus, in 1118 for his Manichaean preachings of the dual nature of man – that he was created by Satan in his image but with the seeds of light within him.

The central tenet of the Cathari ('the Pure'), as the sect's believers were called, was that God had created the Spirit, and the Devil had made the material world which included Adam. Hence this world was evil and Eve, as the embodiment of sensual seduction, was the symbol of corruption. Because man embodies the Spirit of God within the Devil's body a conflict is in progress between the angels of light and the demons for possession of mankind. When all the particles of captive light and all the just souls have been set free the world will be consumed by fire. Hence it was the duty of believers to eschew the pleasures of the flesh and to censure all forms of uncleanness so that their soul might escape its fleshy prison.

According to the Cathari the Catholic Church had sinned by misinterpreting the nature of creation. Borrowing from earlier Gnostic philosophy, they held that Christ was the second son of God, composed of spirit and a non-material though visible body. In spite of their fastidious avoidance of the unclean, it is said that some of these groups allowed orgiastic rituals for young initiates before imposing the strict disciplines of their faith – rather like a stag party! Such orgies may have some connection with certain eastern Tantric practices which used sex as a means of attaining enlightenment, though they may well have been hatched by the over-heated imagination of the participants.

The Manichaean heresy to which St Augustine had subscribed as a young man may well have survived from this time uninterruptedly for seven centuries among other cults of the remote peoples in the hinterlands of Europe, but we have no evidence of it until the twelfth and thirteenth centuries when there was growing contact amongst the nations through trade and the movement of armies on crusade. But certainly its latterday expression in the beliefs of the Cathari found ready followers, especially in the Languedoc area of France where the local nobility were deeply involved in the cult.

Pope Innocent III tried to combat this deep-rooted and

widespread belief by sending missionaries into France, particularly his 'Inquisitor-General' St Dominic. Finding that the Cathari were in the main a highly intellectual group, St Dominic saw that the only way to convert them was through superior argument. (He founded the Dominican order in 1215 with its emphasis on study and learning.) But in spite of St Dominic's vehement preaching against the Albigenses (Albi was a Cathari stronghold and the heresy came to be called Albigensian) the beliefs persisted and when the papal legate was killed in a local affray, the Pope called for a crusade to rid France once and for all of these heretics. The king of France was too busy defending his frontiers to lead a religious war within his own domain, but he allowed his northern nobles to wage war in his name.

These dukes in the north of France were more than happy to root out heresy in the south for the glory of God, especially since it offered them a splendid opportunity to appropriate the conquered lands for themselves. In 1208 Simon de Montfort led the northern armies with the same brilliance that his more famous son was to show in 1264 at the Battle of Lewes against Henry III. The object of the crusade was accomplished successfully, in a style characteristic of most crusades: the complete and bloody annihilation of the heathen. So heavy was the slaughter in one Languedoc town that the papal legate had to justify it on the grounds that all the souls would go before God and the guilty would be condemned and the innocent forgiven. Those who did not die in battle were tortured and burned to rid them of their beliefs. All palpable signs of the Cathari were stamped out in this crusade, but their ideas were kept alive in secret and many of their principles have survived down to our own times in certain religious groups like the Church of the Final Judgment. And for many centuries western China supported a powerful Manichaean church far removed from the persecutions of Rome.

The tragic fate of the Albigensian heretics throws into sharp relief the confusion that existed in the orthodox Church of the twelfth century. As a fervent Catholic how did one deal with heresy? By intellectual conversion or by the sword? The uncertainties of religious experience gave rise to new movements started by visionaries and teachers within the Church who sought the direct blessing of the Pope himself rather than attempting to earn the approval of his bishops, who were more interested in playing politics than saving souls. Prominent among them was the reformer of the nunneries of Europe, St Hildegarde of Bingen and Sts Francis and Dominic who respectively founded the Franciscan and Dominican orders. The object of St Hildegarde's society was to minister to the poverty-stricken. The Pope gave his blessing to her order and she rose to a position of prominence in the Catholic hierarchy. St Hildegarde was sent on a tour of the nunneries in western Europe with the idea of reforming them. Her visits were timely indeed since many of the nuns interpreted their vow of never marrying as a means of taking lovers rather than husbands. The bewildered Abbess gently remonstrated with them and brought them back into the fold with a few disciplinary prayers.

St Hildegarde travelled widely through Europe preaching and teaching a return to the true faith, buttressed in her belief by the visions she had seen warning her of future catastrophes to be visited upon a faithless world. When the two religious orders were founded at the beginning of the thirteenth century the Knights Templars had already been flourishing for nearly one hundred years. In 1118 nine French knights had bound themselves together to protect pilgrims on their way to the Holy Land; they attracted other gallant knights to their ranks who maintained the hospices and built a chain of castles across Europe to Jerusalem. In spite of their self-styled title as the 'Poor Soldiers of the Holy City' the order became very wealthy and corrupt, exciting the envy and suspicion of kings and bishops, since, like the Friars, they were responsible only to the Pope. For this reason the Knights Templars became a secret society which led to their being accused of fraternizing with heathens and following their ways, of keeping concubines and worshipping an imaginary idol called Baphomet (a corruption of Mohammed).

The only possible evidence of such heresy is some bizarre carvings in a few of their buildings which are no more damning than the gargoyles on any Catholic church of the time. But in 1312 the Pope succumbed to the pleas of the king of France, Philip the Handsome, and suppressed the order. Many of the Knights joined the Order of St John of Jerusalem, but their last Grand Master, Jacques de Molay, was sentenced to death at the stake.

The western world in the thirteenth century was obsessively preoccupied with heresy and how to root it out. Religious refugees fled the tyranny of episcopal oppression and took refuge within the more tolerant borders of the Islamic empire. Rabbi Moses ben Maimon (Maimonides), one of the greatest Jewish philosophers and teachers, was driven out of Muslim Spain and took refuge in Egypt where he became personal physician to its ruler Caliph Saladin. Under the protection of Saladin Maimonides organized Jewish religious literature and through his work

left The Cathedral at Albi, centre of the Albigensian heresy. This Manichaean belief was suppressed by a crusade led by Simon de Montfort under circumstances of extreme cruelty.

above Jacques de Molay, the last Grand Master of the Knights Templars, and three of his followers burnt at the stake in 1312. Fifteenth-century Flemish manuscript.

above A holy well in Wales. Now a wishing well this spring was used in the sixth century by St Seirol to baptise his converts.

brought about a golden age of scientific enlightenment in the study of the scriptures. Eschewing Maimonides' rational, anti-mystic philosophy, other rabbis began studying the meaning of biblical prophesies by giving each letter a number: from this they advanced to mystical interpretation of the scriptures. While in Prague, Rabbi Judah Loew was said to have known the words of creation which gave him the power to create the Golem, an artificial human form which served all his needs. Though the story is apocryphal it shows that the Jews did not confine themselves to following the rationalism of Maimonides but also supported the idea of a type of magic based on a numerology of words.

Towards the end of the thirteenth century, when the crusading spirit had exhausted itself, international commerce took its place. Merchant-adventurers like Marco Polo, who had been an adviser to the Tartar emperor of China, Kublai Khan, returned to Venice with new ideas from the east, as well as eastern stories of magic. The trade routes opened up a passage by which the gipsies entered Europe from India; and the Tarot cards may similarly have found their way into Italy at this time, although their origin is obscure.

The Tarot cards had their own magic markings and gave an expression and an impetus to one of the most important oriental influences in the development of the occult: the use of symbols and diagrams in the practice of ceremonial magic. Although mostly Arabic or Jewish in origin, many of these symbolic designs came from the rituals of alchemy which started in Egypt, grew under the Roman Empire and were brought back to western Europe through the teachings of Arab scholars.

One of the most curious and terrible stories to emerge from the later Middle Ages concerns a Constable of France, Gilles de Rais. A young homosexual of considerable wealth and a favourite of the king, de Rais was accused by his enemies in 1440 of having murdered a hundred and forty children in the most diabolical rituals of ceremonial magic. Only one dismembered corpse, however, was presented as evidence. Implicated with him were a chaplain and chamberlain of his household, both of whom confessed under torture to obscene rites, necrophilia and the placing of a decapitated head in a bowl of blood to make an oracle. Gilles de Rais confessed to enlisting the aid of the Devil to bring him gold and to gain more power and social importance. As one of the richest and most powerful men in France there was little more wealth or influence he could have wished! The whole trial testimony reads like a Gothic horror story and although the evidence was unsatisfactory by our standards, circumstantially it seems damning enough. De Rais capped it all by a public confession of frightful happenings, such as offering the Devil a chalice filled with the eyes and tongues of murdered boys. The upshot of this most disagreeable trial was that the two accomplices were given death sentences in accordance with their social degree while the noble de Rais was strangled in private and his body shown to the public.

Gilles de Rais the military commander was a contemporary of Joan of Arc who was accused by the English of witchcraft. While the Constable of France was said to be a necromancer and magician, Joan was believed to be a witch: to the contemporary mind the two crimes were poles apart.

Joan, an illiterate country girl, heard the voice of an archangel bidding her to save France. The king gave her command of the army and having raised the siege of Orleans she conducted Charles to his coronation at Rheims.

left The burning of Joan of Arc in the public square at Rouen. One of the charges against her was that she had listened to spirit voices in her youth. Nineteenth-century engraving.
below A modern reconstruction of the same scene from the French film 'Passion de Jeanne d'Arc'.

In 1430 she was taken prisoner by the Burgundians and handed over to the English. Joan tried to escape from prison but she broke her arm in a fall and was recaptured; she interpreted this as a divine punishment for doubting that her fate was in the hands of God as revealed by his angel. At the French ecclesiastical court – with the help of the Inquisition – she was sentenced to burn as a witch. Her heart, it is said, would not burn and it had to be thrown in the Seine.

What of the charge of witchcraft? Joan was found guilty of wearing men's clothes and her voices were said to be not those of angels but of demons. She had heard her voices since childhood in Domremy on the borders of Champagne and Lorraine – true Celtic country with a tradition of holy springs, lucky wells and fairy voices. She was clearly no worshipper of ancient gods – by the time she was thirteen her voices were identified with Christian saints. Four years later she set out on her mission. The concept of Joan's 'witchcraft' was a reaction by intellectuals of the Church who could not support the idea of a peasant girl leading an army – therefore, they argued, the Devil must have been at work.

Joan's trial was conducted at a time when the fear of Satan loomed large over Europe, and the Pope and ecclesiastical councils denounced breakaway religious groups with sanctimonious dispatch, fully believing they were keeping the lid firmly on Hell. One such group called the Beghards was formed by a priest of Liège, Lambert le Bègue ('the Stammerer') in the Low Countries early in the thirteenth century. The Beghards initiated the beguine sisterhoods, whose members did not have to take religious vows. By the fourteenth century many such uncommitted groups were drifting into heresy and the Inquisition pointed an accusing finger at them.

The Flemish people called the Beghards Lollards ('the Mutterers'), a term of opprobrium which came to be applied to any group of independent thinkers of the period. In Britain the followers of John Wycliffe (1320–84) earned the name by their endeavours to have the revenues of the Church put to secular uses.

Wycliffe, a great scholar and reformer, launched a determined attack on the papacy and was banned by Pope Gregory XI, which only led him to declare that the papacy was 'Antichrist himself'. He went on to deny the doctrine of transubstantiation, and to assert the right of every man to read the Bible for himself. To this end he instituted the first English translation of the Bible. But his denial of transubstantiation was regarded as heresy by many of his

left Gilles de Rais, Constable of France, arraigned and executed for child murder. He allegedly used the corpses in his ritual magic ceremonies.

above The popular sixteenth-century concept of witches working their spells. Engraving by Hans Baldung, 1510.

colleagues, who refused to associate with him. Condemned by an ecclesiastical court, he was not sentenced to the usual fate of the heretic as he suffered a series of strokes which finally killed him. His bones were dug up half a century later, burnt and thrown into a tributary of the Avon.

But Wycliffe's ideas on the corruption of the Church were propagated by the Lollards and they found their most vigorous expression in the writings of John Huss, the impassioned leader of the Hussite Movement in Bohemia. Driven out of Prague by order of the Bohemian king and his bishops Huss continued to preach against the corruption of the official Church of Bohemia. But when the Council of Constance, convened by the Church in 1415, ruled that

right Condemned heretics are offered a
last chance to recant; those who refused
were garotted on the pyres and burnt. From
Picart's book, 'Religious Ceremonies' 1731.

Wycliffe's teachings were heretical and works of the Devil,
Huss refused to recant. He was burnt at the stake and his
ashes scattered to the four winds. His death was the signal
for a nationalistic uprising among the Czechs under John
Ziska who gained many victories over the armies of the
Holy Roman Empire. (Ziska, incidentally, ordered that
after his death his skin be made into a drumhead.) The
triumphant Hussite cause carried the Church before it and
Bohemia remained a dissident body of Christians for two
centuries. John Huss's writings were to have a profound
influence on Martin Luther.

Behind all the theological disputes across Europe the
folk beliefs and customs continued, as we can see from the
written evidence of the prosecutors of witches and heretics.
Curiously, the official ecclesiastical attitude towards heresy
did not differentiate between its various manifestations –
whether it be blasphemy, occult practices, eastern mysticism or whatever – it was all labelled as witchcraft, in
other words Devil-worship. And witchcraft by definition
was performed by thirteen individuals organized into
covens with link men co-ordinating their activities. The
name 'witch' derives from the old English 'wicca' the same
word that gives us 'wicked'.

Ways of combating this evil were debated within the
Church and several treatises were published, culminating
in the text-book of its day, *Malleus Maleficarum*, ('The
Hammer of the Witches'). It was published in 1484 by
Jakob Sprenger and Heinrich Kramer, two Dominican
Friars commissioned to investigate the heresy of witchcraft. The book attributes all evil-doing to the inspiration
of Satan and describes in loving detail how witches can be
discovered (including some most obscene tortures) and
how they should be punished. The Friars, believing it their
Christian duty to eradicate witchcraft once and for all,
indulged themselves shamelessly in suggesting excessive
tortures and retributions. Torture, insisted Sprenger,
should be continued on successive days, children could
denounce their parents, and defending lawyers should be
suspect themselves.

A gradual process of change blurred the dying years of the Middle Ages. The opening up of the Far East, the expansion of trade across Europe and the pilgrimages to Catholic shrines had broadened people's horizons as well as increasing their wealth. With the spread of education accepted tenets of religion were questioned, and Christianity as taught by the Friars showed that there was a yawning gap between the conduct of contemporary Church leaders and that of the disciples of the Gospels. The peasants began to flex their political muscles and revolts broke out like a rash all over Europe. In England the serfs demanded a penny a day to spend as they wished.

By the fifteenth century the high point of civilization and wealth had been reached in the Italian trading cities of Florence, Pisa and Bologna, outstripping the magnificence of Islamic cultural centres. The artistic rivalry among the great ducal houses produced public works and private palaces of ostentatious elegance and beauty. Life was sweet for the aristocracy of Renaissance Italy and they indulged their senses in paintings, costumes and jewellery to the point of creating a cult of exquisite paganism, a religion of material beauty.

A backlash against the artistic licence and social corruption of the Renaissance was inevitable: in 1494 a religious reaction was set off when a Dominican monk, Fra Girolamo Savonarola began preaching against the idle luxury of life in Florence. His message of simple living and of charity struck a chord in the hearts of the people and his warnings of disaster seemed all the more imminent when the French king Charles VIII invaded Italy. Savonarola favoured a political alliance with the French and after his most powerful opponents, the Medici family, had been expelled he became leader of the democratic party. By his political agreement with Charles Savonarola aroused the emnity of Pope Alexander VI, but the people adored the pious monk and his eloquent preaching drew them to his Christian

Chapter Five

THE *Devil* LET *Loose*

message. Children marched in the streets praising God and the rich sent cartloads of fine clothes and ornaments to be burnt. For a while Florence rejoiced in the ideals of Christianity, but in 1497 the Pope excommunicated Savonarola for allying himself with the French and he was executed as a heretic. Evangelism and politics were an explosive mixture in Renaissance Italy.

Savonarola had relied on the persuasiveness of his sermons but the most powerful weapon in the battle for men's minds in the fifteenth century was the printing press. This new invention ensured that the ideas of scholars could be widely disseminated. One of the most influential of the early religious tracts was written by the Augustinian monk, Thomas à Kempis (1380–1471). *De Imitatione Christi* traced the gradual process of the soul to Christian perfection, its detachment from the sybaritic world of bishops and princes and its union with God. The thoughts of a monk who seems never to have left his cloister were later translated into many languages and their simplicity and sincerity had a universal appeal.

Printing also meant that existing works could be studied more readily, both those of the classical writers and the older texts of the Bible. When Byzantium fell to the Turks in 1453 the scholars of the eastern Church had brought their ancient manuscripts to the west, giving great impetus to the study of the classics in Italy. The movement of Byzantine scholars into Europe was counterbalanced by the expulsion of the Moors from Spain in 1492 which brought to an end the great Islamic civilization there. The Spanish Inquisition was established fourteen years earlier – a retrograde step into bigotry and intolerance at a time when the accumulated knowledge and wisdom of the east had become available to western intellectuals.

In France and Italy the old black-letter typography gave way to classical type-faces and wonderful wood-block illustrations. The Aldine Press in Venice produced such elegant works as *The Dream of Polyphilio*, a romance by Pico della Mirandola, with its drawings of the court of Venus in renaissance costume. Two-faced human forms are depicted emerging from trees, providing a hint of witchcraft cults to suggest that readers of the classical authors were beginning to rediscover the secret country practices of the past.

left Death and Life dance hand in hand. The maid and her knight are taken away. Death the leveller strips the Bishop of his symbols of power leaving him naked on his tomb. An echo of the tragedy of the Black Death in a fifteenth-century 'Book of Hours'.

upper left The Dance of Death : a series of sixteenth-century woodcuts after Holbein. The astrologer consults the celestial globe but fails to note that Death has called for him.
left Even as the Usurer takes his profit Death decides that his hour has come.
above Death the garlanded conquerer leads the Old Woman to the grave.
right The mighty Emperor is taken at the height of his power.

When Martin Luther nailed his ninety-five theses to the door of St Peter's Church in Wittenberg in 1512, he was challenging the corruption of the sixteenth-century Catholic Church. The immediate cause of the young Augustinian monk's fury was the sale of papal indulgences by which sinners could be spared purgatorial suffering in return for money. In 1520 a papal bull was promulgated against him. Luther appealed to the German nobility for protection and gained the support of his own feudal lord, Frederick the Wise of Saxony. But when Luther questioned the validity of the sacraments of the Church he had, in the eyes of Rome, passed over to the Devil's side. Summoned before the Diet of Worms in April 1521, he was excommunicated. He left the monastic order, married Catherine von Bora and devoted himself to forming the League of Protestantism. But for all his reforming zeal, Luther sided with the establishment against the peasants in their revolt of 1525. The revolt frittered out in a gruesome catalogue of torture and murder.

The effects of wider literacy and the availability of the printed word guaranteed more support for the efforts of reformers like Luther. In the popular movements for reform of the Church the nobles found an ideal opportunity for seizing its wealth and curbing its influence. Hence the Reformation saw the Church more bitterly divided than at any time in its history. It was not the undermining effects of the old primitive religions but the free-thinking tradition of the Renaissance that shook Christendom.

The Catholic Church recognized the need to set its house in order. For eighteen years the Council of Trent deliberated on how best to counter this new spirit of reform which came from outside the Church. A new catechism was published in 1566 and in the following year the *Index Expurgatorius* – a list of banned books – was issued. The text of the Vulgate version of the Bible was carefully edited and the Jesuits, authorized by a papal bull of 1540, began a missionary effort to re-evangelize Europe and the rest of the world back to Catholicism.

While the Spanish Inquisition continued on its bloody road, religious teachers and reformers travelled through Europe preaching a simple doctrine, a return to the basic truths of the Gospels. Such a one was St Teresa of Avila, a mystic visionary and an energetic reformer who belonged to the Carmelite Order. During her devotions she was liable to float gently to the ceiling of the church and remain there for some time, much to the astonishment of her sister nuns. In contrast, her writings show her to be a practical woman who administered her convents purposefully and

below Florentine tragedy : the execution of Fra Girolamo Savonarola and his companions. As an act of grace they had been hanged before being burnt. From a painting in the Church of San Marco, Florence.
right Portrait of Savonarola. Having led the people of Florence to destroy their worldly treasures he became their political leader. With the return of the Medicis he was abandoned by the people and executed. Painting by Fra Bartolomeo in the Church of San Marco, Florence.
below right Jerome of Prague. A follower of Huss, sentenced to death as a heretic he was burnt at Constance in 1416. He wears a headdress showing demons which were thought would seize his soul as he died.

below The fall of Abbot Theophilus of Silistria. To obtain victory in a dispute with his Bishop the Abbot pledged his soul to Satan. He is shown signing away his salvation before the court of Hell. From a French manuscript of the 'Miracles of Our Lady', painted in 1456.

with great understanding. St Teresa was also aware of the world around her and she kept in constant touch with her brother who was away fighting wild Indian tribes in Paraguay. She was friendly with the Spanish mystical poet and Friar of the Carmelite Order, St John of the Cross whose works on meditation remain a guide today.

Unfortunately it was not the simple piety of the saints, both Catholic and Protestant, which prevailed during the Reformation, but the political machinations of kings, popes and princes of the Church. To the zealous the existence of the Devil was as real as that of God and naturally they would see the Devil's hand guiding the actions of their enemies. The Protestants with their simple severity believed the ceremonies of Catholic worship to be diabolically inspired; their leader the Pope was Antichrist himself. The peasants saw that the bishop was hand in glove with the prince to keep them working the land and exact taxes; the Reformers offered them a release from exploitation.

On the other hand the Catholics held that the Reformers, especially in their teaching against the seven sacraments, were seducing believers away from the only true religion. The peasantry in Catholic regions, finding themselves suddenly under a Protestant princeling as a result of some local war, regretted the loss of the colourful rituals of Catholicism which had brought some richness into their dreary lives. They were attached to their saints and to the quarterly ceremonies denounced by the Reformers as heathenish abominations. The practitioners of magic fell between the two warring religious groups: witches and devil-worshippers were supposedly discovered everywhere and subjected to tortures and lingering deaths.

Monarchy chose the side best suited to its political and economic purposes. To Henry VIII in England the Reformers offered a way out of his matrimonial difficulties. Proof that Henry's attitude towards the new Protestantism was purely pragmatic can be seen in his ordering the noble Sir Thomas More, the Chancellor of England, to the scaffold for his refusal to repudiate the authority of the Pope, while at the same time sending wretched Protestants to the stake for denying the doctrine of transubstantiation. Yet the new religion appealed to the people when they realized it meant an end to the rule of Rome; and for Henry the monasteries with their land and riches were too great a temptation to resist. With the destruction of the monasteries came the desecration of shrines of the saints, including that of Thomas à Becket at Canterbury before whose remains Henry had once knelt in prayer.

Throughout Europe Catholic princes fought Protestant princes as much for self-aggrandizement and territorial gain as for their creed. The Holy Roman Empire, now ruled by a Hapsburg emperor, remained Catholic while the northern nations espoused the Protestant cause. Reading of the political wars of the Reformation it is as hard to find the name of an honest man as it is to find the

below The burning of Thomas Bilney from Fox's 'Book of Martyrs'. A Protestant victim of the Catholic revival in England during the reign of Queen Mary.

74

name of a village which was not sacked in the name of God and its population raped and hanged.

Each side had its propogandists, men of learning, the children of the Renaissance who kept the torch of scholarship alight in those dark years. Like the ignorant peasants who maintained the ancient cults throughout the Middle Ages and were now being hounded out and burnt or drowned as witches, these philosophers and artists went about their business creating a new Humanist literature out of the remains of classical art and ideas. What Dante and Petrarch had begun in the heart of the Middle Ages by delving back into Latin literature, writers like Erasmus and Thomas More sustained in the sixteenth century.

With the re-awakened interest in classicism ancient magical practices were revived, especially the use of geometric diagrams and squares of Pythagoras. (In the British Museum are the magical wax tablets of Dr John Dee, Queen Elizabeth I's astrologer, which are covered with precise geometric diagrams and symbols.) We can appreciate how closely linked philosophy and magic were at the time of the Reformation by the work of Paracelsus or, to give him his full name, Philippus Aureolus Theophrastus Bombastus Ab Hohenheim (1493–1541). Paracelsus came from a poor family in Schwaben where folk-medicine and magic were much practised; he wandered from country to country studying at the universities and practising magic, alchemy and astrology, yet he was never granted a degree. Paracelsus did not suffer fools gladly; the blinkered humbug of the academics outraged him and his nervous irascibility created many enemies.

He settled in Germany where he effected many remarkable cures employing traditional country medicine, and as a result was appointed to the chair of physic and surgery at the University of Basel. There he developed a great interest in alchemy and ceremonial magics which he studied with his friend Cornelius Agrippa, the scholar and writer on the occult. From his researches Paracelsus discovered much about the medicinal effects of chemicals and has been called the father of modern chemistry. After publicly burning the works of Galen and Avicenna as inferior to his own, Paracelsus was pronounced a quack and he fled from Basel, wandering once more until his death in Salzburg.

Although Paracelsus used magic potions on his patients, he worked to rationalize the science of medicine and he believed that the healer must not only treat that part of the body which is sick, but must restore the balance of health to the whole person. All his life he taught that nature was one vast unity – the result of a divine plan which would

left The Arts of the Devil. Demons are cast out from the terrestial orb into the jaws of Hell. Satan sends out two emissaries to tempt mankind. They practise their subversion by whispering lustful thoughts into the ears of lovers.
above The martyrdom of St Edmund at the hands of the heathen Norsemen.

eventually be understood by mankind through God-given intellect.

Another intellectual outsider was Giordano Bruno (1548–1600), a Dominican Friar who developed a pantheistic philosophy for which he was drummed out of his order. He wandered from university to university teaching that God is the unity reconciling spirit and matter, hence all nature is one – a highly unpalatable thesis for the clergy, who saw to it that the Inquisition were informed of Bruno's heresy. The philosopher was burnt alive in February 1600. But the central idea of his teaching was borrowed by the occultists who reasoned that if nature is a unity then events in one phase can be controlled by actions in another. For instance, a man born under the sign of Venus could be able to influence anything that is particularly related to that sign by concentrating his mind on it.

To the superstitious mind of the sixteenth century men like Paracelsus and Bruno were open to the suspicion of having sold their souls to the Devil in return for mysterious powers. Such men, working apart in their laboratories, were believed to be assisted by necromancers and evil wizards who helped them to harm their neighbours or extract knowledge from revivified corpses. Rumour had it that Paracelsus had been seen in four different places at the same time and that he was followed everywhere by a familiar spirit in the shape of a black dog. It was popularly supposed that this creature ran away with his soul when he died after a tavern brawl. Even the sword that Paracelsus wore – out of a nervous habit – was believed to have magic properties. The iron blade kept spirits at bay, it was said, and so protected the alchemical elixir of life which he secreted in the pommel.

While the university intellectuals in the towns were exposed to accusations of trafficking with the Devil, groups of countryfolk were able to practise ancient magical rituals in their worship of a horned god whom many of them believed to be Satan. They had seen paintings of him on the walls of their churches. He was in fact a much older creation – the Lord of the Wildwood, the Power of Nature, Cernunnos, whose partner was the Moon Goddess.

'I would have no pity on these witches; I would burn them all.' Thus wrote Martin Luther in his *Table Talk*. And with the Reformation witch-hysteria reached its peak. Catholic and Protestant accused each other of being witches in the sense that they worshipped Satan and ensnared the immortal souls of their converts to serve the powers of Hell. Witch-fever did cross the channel into England, but it was on the Continent that the infection spread like plague, claiming thousands of innocent victims, especially in Germany where two hundred witches were publicly burnt in the Rhineland within a week. One writer suggests that a hundred thousand witches were burnt in Germany alone in the seventeenth century.

Often people reached a state of hysterical depression in which they accused themselves and their families of witch-craft and after the customary tests (the ducking stool, or 'swimming', where the suspect is lowered by rope into a river: if she floated she was a witch, if she did not she was innocent but drowned anyway), followed by the obligatory tortures; then the public hanging or burning. It was a terrible phase of human history and the victims were mostly poor peasant women handed over to the torturers and executioners by their own priests and parsons.

If the religious wars of the sixteenth and seventeenth centuries created witch-fever they also were responsible for the marked increase in the practice of alchemy. War-lords needed gold to raise armies. Mexican and Peruvian gold financed the Inquisition's activities in the Low Countries and the oppressions of other Catholic rulers, but the Protestant princes had to rely on taxes and booty. They turned in desperation to the alchemists in the hope of finding a new source of gold.

The study of alchemy was motivated by a religious philosophy similar to that of the pantheist Bruno – that spirit and matter are intimately connected in the oneness of Creation. Therefore one material can be transmuted into another. Taking lead as the base metal, by refining it and amalgamating it with other metals it can be turned into mercury and then into gold – the purest of all substances, according to the adepts. The hypothesis is not far removed from our atomic theory, for if one could add a ring of electrons to the lead atom, mercury would result, and another ring of electrons to the atomic structure of mercury would produce gold. (There is evidence in the British Museum today of gold having been produced from lead!)

In the process of transmutation volatile spirits were distilled off, the quintessence of which was thought to be the elixir of life, a panacea capable of curing all illness. Paracelsus admonished the alchemists of his day for wasting their time in their search for gold rather than concentrating on the elixir.

The alchemists' quest was for the philosopher's stone by which the transmutations could be made. Descriptions vary – some say it was a waxy substance of high specific gravity, others a heavy red powder. But the search for this inestimable treasure by alchemists produced much scientific knowledge quite accidentally. Bötticher stumbled on the manufacture of Dresden porcelain; Roger Bacon on the composition of gunpowder; Geber on the properties of acids; Van Helmont on the nature of gas; and Dr Glauber on the 'salts' which bear his name.

Certainly the alchemists seem to have been protected from the horrors of the Inquisition and only to have fallen foul of it if there was any reason – other than the quest for the philosopher's stone – to suspect them of heresy. But scientists in the seventeenth century not engaged in alchemy were less fortunate. Galileo saw spots on the sun and when he innocently mentioned the fact he was accused

below The Propaganda of hatred at the
time of the Reformation. Here Satan is
shown using the Reformer Martin Luther
as the windbag for his pipe music.

left The Fortress of the Faith. Perhaps a riposte to Luther's Hymn, 'Fin Feste Burg'. The religious orders, the Pope and Bishops hold the fortress against the assults of heretical preachers and the impious. Fifteenth-century Flemish miniature from Bruges.

above Paracelsus (1493–1541), philosopher, astrologer, alchemist and healer. This woodcut from the 1570 edition of his book 'Archidoxa' shows the alchemical symbol on his sword pommel which led people to believe it contained a specimen of the Philosopher's Stone.

universe or that the planets had moons. The serfs were too preoccupied with their ceremonial observance of the seasons and in maintaining their health and strength to combat plague to worry their heads over the intellectual 'heresies' of philosophers. When they fell ill they consulted the wise woman of their village who was as well equipped to administer a medicinal concoction of frogs' eyes and boiled newt as any court doctor; and besides the wise woman knew her patients.

As a midwife the wise woman had probably assisted at their birth; she had watched them grow, healing their cuts with spider's webs, drawing their boils with special poultices. She could probably charm warts away by reciting a rhyming verse over them. (Or she might employ the traditional cure for warts prescribed by Marcellus of Bordeaux in the fourth century AD: touch your warts with as many stones as you have warts; then wrap the stones in an ivy leaf and cast them out into the road. Whoever picks up the parcel of stones will get the warts and you will lose them.)

The villagers trusted their wise woman, but they shunned certain hermit-like neighbours, old and bad-tempered, who were more likely to pronounce a curse on a stranger than a greeting. Antisocial behaviour was considered sinister in the sixteenth and seventeenth centuries and if a lonely cantankerous old woman kept a cat or a dog for company it was assumed to be her familiar and she a witch. Accusations against witches in Britain invariably centred around their leaguing together to cause accidents to those who had crossed them. In farming communities such accidents were bound to happen to cattle, crops and the milk yield. If any groups of such people came together it is quite possible that their combined telepathic power did produce some results, but the crimes were more often than not pathetic when compared to the accusations of murder and poisoning which fill Continental casebooks.

How far Tudor England believed in magic can be seen in the plays of Shakespeare, which reflect many of the fashionable superstitions. The humorous and melancholic Jacques of *As You Like It* gives the impression that he knows where to worship the old gods of the Forest of Arden. Ghosts like Hamlet's father, the fairies of *Midsummer Night's Dream*, the mysterious Herne the Hunter (the horned Celtic Cernunnos) of *Merry Wives of Windsor*, the caskets of alchemical metals in *The Merchant of Venice* all show the breadth and currency of magic beliefs – to say nothing of Macbeth's witches. But perhaps Shakespeare's most convincing statement of magic is his last play, *The*

of heresy: the sun was a symbol of God and how could there be imperfections in the Creator! Galileo was thrown into prison by an obscurantist Church which refused to acknowledge the scientific proof of his theories.

If men like Galileo were vilified by the Church, the mass of the people were completely ignorant of their scientific pronouncements. It was of little importance to the farm labourer that the earth was no longer the centre of the

far left The examination of a suspected sorcerer. The magistrate listens with severity as he watches his clerk question the suspect under torture and record the answers.
left Execution of a sorcerer in Germany in 1517. The victim's limbs have been lascerated by the wheel, while the witch is carried away by the Devil.
below The execution of witches in the Rhineland in 1555. The Devil seizes the soul of one witch as she dies in the flames. Thousands of alleged witches perished in this manner during an hysterical outburst of witch-fever throughout Germany in the sixteenth century.

left A page from 'Alchemie de Flamel' a seventeenth-century French manuscript, said to be a copy of the Book of Abraham the Jew. The Tree of Knowledge grows again bearing the Philosopher's Stone as its fruit. The alchemical metals and the planets are shown as mystic birds and beasts.
below A fourteenth-century Italian herbalist collects medicinal plants.
bottom The laboratory of a seventeenth-century Dutch Alchemist. From a painting by David Teniers.

Tempest. The exiled magician Prospero on the island of the banished witch Sycorax conjures various spirits, including Ariel, to his service. Caliban, the misshapen monster and son of the witch could conceivably be Shakespeare's concept of the Golem, the artificial human slave.

Clearly Shakespeare's audience were thoroughly grounded in magic lore – not the arcane precepts of the occultists and philosophers but the ancient lore of the countryside. Puck in *Midsummer Night's Dream* is referred to as Robin Goodfellow, the 'shrewd and knavish sprite' – a practical-joking elf known to the Scots as a Brownie, the Germans as *Kobold* and the Scandinavians as *Nisse God-dreng*. Oberon and Titania, the King and Queen of the Fairies, could pronounce sweet blessings and in that wood 'not far from Athens' all is alive – this is late Tudor romanticism half believing in pre-Christian cults.

Yet this widespread acceptance of fairies and ghosts did not take the edge off the business of witch-hunting. The public execution of witches was even more popular than bear-baiting or cock-fighting. In England and on the Continent the citizenry thronged to watch the holiday spectacle of some old crone gasping for breath in the ducking stool or dancing at the end of a rope.

With a few notable exceptions those accused of witchcraft were poor, old, lonely people whose ignorance and filthy clothes were so despised by the court that there could be no intellectual contact between the accused and the judge. No one would have dreamt of pointing the finger of suspicion at the intellectual occultists, like John Dee, who enjoyed royal patronage. (Even so on one occasion the populace broke into Dee's house and destroyed most of his valuable collection of mathematical instruments, convinced that he held intercourse with the Devil.) Dee professed to being able to raise the dead and he had a magic mirror in which people could see their friends in distant lands and how they were occupied. The erudite Dr Dee travelled widely on diplomatic missions, in the course of which he conducted occult discussions throughout Europe. On these trips he was accompanied by the reprobate medium Edward Kelly who it is said could summon up spirits which he alone could see. Kelly wrote a rather derivative book on alchemy which shows that he had a keen appreciation for the 'arts magicall'.

Men like Kelly and Dee could happily pursue the occult arts unaffected by the stringent witchcraft laws brought in by Elizabeth in 1563 and James I in 1604, since their field of magic was not considered Satanic; whereas the mass trial of the Pendle Forest witches in August 1612 shows that

upper One of the inscribed wax tablets used by the great Elizabethan occultist Dr John Dee, as a support for the table on which he read his crystal ball.
above Shakespeare's fairies as seen by the Swiss artist Heinrich Füselli (1721–1845) in his painting of Titania and the ass-headed Bottom.

above left The hanging of witches in seventeenth-century England. The executioner has 'topped' four victims. Three more are soon to be hanged. In the right the witch finder receives his wage for the discovery of the coven.
lower left A group of English refugees from religious persecution leave their haven in Holland to found a settlement in Massachusetts 1620.
upper The Salem Witch Trial. One of the possessed children accuses a young woman of casting a witch spell on her. A reconstructed drawing.
above The Reverend Cotton Mather. A respected Minister of Salem, Massachusetts, who was convinced that the outbreak of witchcraft in his town was inspired by Satanic forces.

the old women who cast spells and worked with clay effigies inevitably ended up on the gallows. The feuding witch families of Elizabeth Southern, alias Old Demdike, and Anne Whittle, alias Old Chattox, worked their witchery against each other's clan, cursing their children and cattle to death. At the trial of twenty alleged witches the various family members confessed freely, implicating each other – daughters accusing mothers, and sisters brothers – and telling of their familiar spirits in the shape of dogs, cats and hares. These familiars were devils in animal form who had promised great wealth and power to women who would pledge their souls to them. Ten of the witches were found guilty and hanged.

Their curious confessions – including the murder of a man by piercing a wax image of him with teeth taken from churchyard skulls – and their apparent willingness to be accepted as witches led their contemporaries to suppose that some kind of peasant witch organization really did exist, however absurd the evidence of devils and familiars. Thomas Potts the Clerk of the Court at the Pendle Forest trial, was convinced of everything he had heard, as his account of the trial attests: '[They were] crying out in very violent and outrageous manner, even to the gallows, where they died impenitent (for anything we know).'

So we see that at the very dawning of what was to be called the Age of Reason deep-rooted beliefs of ancient paganism reverberated in the minds of men: witchcraft, ceremonial magic and necromancy continued to be practised in spite of the terrible consequences of discovery.

By the second half of the seventeenth century Christendom was split into two armed camps, each accusing the other of devil-worship. Within these camps was another more subtle division – between the court magicians who went beyond their ceremonial magic and studied astronomy and alchemy, and their country cousins of lowlier estate who conjured the spirits for practical purposes – to cure their friends and harm their enemies.

With Europe divided against itself and the eastern Orthodox Church equally racked with disputes and heresies a new threat appeared on the map: the powerful Ottoman Empire and its Turkish armies advancing to the Vienna Woods. After the spiritual exhaustion of the Reformation and its debilitating wars something new was needed – a new enlightenment, a way of looking at things unaffected by cant and prejudice, believing only what could be proved. In other words, Science.

To The Right HUGH LORD This Table is most Honourable WILLOUGHBY OF PARHAM, humbly inscrib'd

VERITE SANS PEUR

above An astronomical chart showing the constellation Corona Borealis, flanked by Hercules and Bootes.

'But it does move . . .' Galileo's muttered remark was his response to being forced to repudiate the Copernican theory that the earth is not the centre of our universe. It was this scientific challenge to dogmatic belief that coloured the new thinking. A spirit of inquiry had been kindled in the minds of educated men by the beginning of the eighteenth century and they began to question old statements and rediscover facts for themselves. Where the astrologer had sought knowledge from the stars as if they could govern human destiny, the astronomer now attempted to discern the laws by which the stars themselves were governed.

This new approach to knowledge created a mechanistic society based on tests and proofs. Unlike the Greek philosophers with their purely theoretical arguments, the eighteenth-century scientists worked from known facts and with these they conducted their experiments to discover new facts. The new astronomers who saw the solar system as a beautifully balanced gravitational engine had no time for the ancient Babylonian proposition that to be born under the right sign of the Zodiac brought luck and advantage. In those exciting years of discovery no scientist could be expected to devote himself to exploring the manifest tomfoolery of the old, country occultism which persisted largely unhindered on its gentle, unsober way.

As more and more educated people began to keep libraries the market for books expanded. Works of philosophy embodied the new thought yet did not reject the ideas of the old occultists. Some were absorbed into the new cosmology in which the symbols of alchemy were augmented by newly-introduced geometric signs. Philosophy was preoccupied with finding a scientific approach to the problem of man is an expanding universe. Eventually the concept crystallized – Man is the microcosm of the universe.

This idea owed much to the theories of an early seventeenth-century physician and Rosicrucian, Robert Fludd. His work is best known for the beautiful mathematical diagrams relating the human form to arcane philosophical structures and to the observed structure of the solar system. Fludd had been accused of dabbling in magic, but as a medical mystic of the school that looked to the Bible for secret clues to science he seems to have enjoyed the respect implied by a flourishing practice. He also vindicated

Chapter Six
THE Age of Reason

the teachings of the Rosicrucians in a series of papers.

It was characteristic of the intellectuals of that period that they tended to bring together many branches of study and form themselves into secret societies as exclusive and ritualized as the old Greek Eleusinians or the Roman military cults. Hence we know little of the origins of the Rosicrucians. They were first heard of in 1614 as a secret society of mystics and alchemists, but the order was said to have been founded by one Christian Rosenkreuz in the late fifteenth century. Whether in fact such a society existed at that time is not known; the tradition may be a mythical story to account for its origin.

The Rosicrucians defended by Fludd in the early seventeenth century seem to have been moral and religious reformers who covered their views under a cloak of mysticism and alchemy. Their insignia, a cross within a rose, symbolized the search for knowledge within mystical religious doctrines. The influence of their members extended far beyond the order.

But it was the discoveries of the astronomers – men like Tycho Brahe, Kepler, and Copernicus – that stimulated the new thirst for knowledge and created trauma within the hearts and minds of religious men. How could the Church accept that the earth on which Christ had walked was merely one among a galaxy of bodies revolving around a centre point of light? Thus science was to have its martyrs as men like Galileo, refusing to renounce their 'heresies', were thrown into prison.

The ideas for which Galileo was gaoled were disproved by Isaac Newton (1642–1727) when he replaced Copernican astronomy with his theory of gravity. He contended that there is a gravitational relationship between the planets which conditions their distance from the sun. Yet he, the greatest scientific mathematician of his day, was deeply involved in occult studies of biblical numerology. He enlarged his idea of a universe to include a search for an order in the sequence of events and the inner realities of heaven.

Newton was indeed the embodiment of the new age, but he was also inescapably the product of the long tradition of belief that preceded him – that the mysteries of the universe can be unlocked by the study of numbers. This aspect of Newton's scientific mysticism relates back to Fludd through one of the most engaging of the Rosi-

above The Gateway of Eternal Wisdom in the Mountain of Philosophers as described by the seventeenth-century mystic and Rosicrucian Heinrich Khunrath. At the end of his intellectual quest the philosopher ascends the stairway to the true light of wisdom.

crucians, Kenelm Digby (1603–65), the man who discovered that plant life needed oxygen to survive. Digby was educated at Oxford and travelled widely. In Madrid he met Charles I and the Duke of Buckingham and through the influence of powerful friends and his own great personal charm he rose rapidly in the social ranks and was knighted.

As a naval commander Digby defeated the French and Venetian fleets in Scanderoon harbour in 1628 and captured a sizeable fortune from Barbary pirates. On his return to England he devoted himself to the study of alchemy. Converted to Catholicism, he tried to persuade Charles I to rally the English Catholics to the Royalist cause, for which he was condemned by Parliament and imprisoned. When he was released in 1643 he fled to France where he made many friends among society and the intelligentsia.

During his time in exile he suddenly developed extraordinary healing powers. The bandages of diseased patients were brought to him and he used to sprinkle them with a vitriol powder. Invariably the patient recovered! There was no apparent scientific explanation for this long-distance medicine; Digby, his contemporaries believed, was using the ancient secrets of alchemy. By 1660 we find him back in London and a member of the Philosophical Society which was granted its royal charter by Charles II two years later, and flourished as the Royal Society for the Advancement of Science.

Whatever Digby's secret healing agent may have been, medicine in the age of enlightenment was frequently no more than a piece of magical hocus-pocus. The majority of people were not within reach of a trained doctor and they looked to the country wise folk, the witches and wizards, for cures. In addition to herbal concoctions and charms the country healers gave their patients symbols to help them over their indispositions. A moorhen's foot, for instance, was prescribed for those who suffered from cramp. The flexibility of the moorhen's foot was supposed to bring its own quality to the sufferer.

People do not denounce the doctor who cures their ailments, so few country healers were implicated in the rash of witch trials throughout Europe of the mid-seventeenth century. The Restoration of the monarchy in England in 1660 brought with it a steady awakening to the absurdity of the alleged power of witches. Actual indictments for witchcraft diminished and between 1662 and 1674 there were no executions as a result of convictions for witchcraft alone. Not so in Europe, where in areas of France and Germany the merciless trials continued. The Mayor of Bamberg was accused of being a warlock and after

above The scientific attitude: Sir Isaac Newton uses a glass prism to demonstrate the properties of sunlight.
below Johann Kepler (1571–1630). His astronomical laws formed the basis of Newton's work and are the starting point of modern astronomy.

prolonged torture was burnt at the stake. A letter, still extant, which he had smuggled out to his daughter tells how he confessed to the charge just to have an end to the torture. In Lorraine the peasants involved in these trials were regularly admonished to confess that they had trafficked with the Devil so that their souls might be saved from everlasting torment. Many screamed false confessions as the torturer approached with red-hot pincers, denouncing friend and foe alike so they too would share the same fate. Accusations and punishments were still based on the fifteenth-century text-book *Malleus Maleficarum* and solid evidence was inevitably lacking.

Accusations of witchcraft in the seventeenth century generally hinged upon supposed membership of a devil-worshipping organization. As in the case of the Pendle Forest witches the accused were said to have promised their immortal souls to Satan in return for magical powers and happiness in this life. It was held that witches danced together at festivals called Esbats accompanied by demons who took on semi-human forms. In accordance with the traditions of classical art these were thought to appear as fauns and satyrs, though the notion of dancing goats and black dogs was also popular.

On four ceremonial occasions during the year the great Sabbats were held when the Devil himself appeared, so it was thought, usually manifesting himself with a goat's head and horns. He would expose a magnificent, huge penis with which he would pierce the women of the coven causing them both great pain and delight. New members were presented at such times, babies were shown to the Devil and named for him, animal sacrifices were made; then all sat down to a sumptuous feast. Following the banquet came the naked orgy, since all witches were supposed to be sexually over-charged and completely without morals.

The sexual aspects of witchcraft had long excited the public imagination. The strictness of the Church's teachings may well have brought about a reaction and even some of the writings of the celibate inquisitors are luridly pornographic in their concentration on sexual questions. Henry Bouguet, in his book *An Examen of Witches* (1590), talks about incubi and succubi, male and female demons who have sexual intercourse with witches, and he solemnly quotes the case of a dog found in a convent who was obviously a devil in disguise!

The celibacy of nuns was always a target for the Devil, according to the popular superstition – a belief that gave rise to one of the most bizarre events of the seventeenth

above Sir Kenelm Digby (1603–1665).
During a self-imposed exile in France to
escape Cromwell's England he performed
inexplicable feats of healing without ever
seeing his patients.

above The village healer – a survival of
early folk-medicine: a nineteenth-century
German engraving showing a wise-woman
falling into a trance to diagnose and cure an
illness.

century, the case of the devils of Loudun. The town's handsome young priest, Urban Grandier, was something of a libertine who acted out the common jokes of the day about priests having intercourse under cover of the confessional and taking willing nuns as his mistresses. Politically Grandier fell foul of his bishop and of Cardinal Richelieu, and soon the devils began to plague the nuns of Loudon. Their adoration for the priest manifested itself in naked homosexual orgies, in which they exhibited all the medieval symptoms of demonic possession, screaming blasphemies and throwing fits.

There is evidence, however, that the nuns were persuaded to campaign against Grandier by higher authority. The Mother Superior of the convent was herself something of a sexual pervert whose example led the nuns into wilder excesses. The inevitable result was the trial of Urban Grandier for witchcraft, charged with causing the Devil to take possession of the bodies of the women concerned. In 1634 he was found guilty and after being horribly tortured he was burnt. But the possessions and fits in the nunnery did not altogether cease with the priest's death. They erupted from time to time for a generation after. The most likely explanation is that the imitation trances induced in the minds of the nuns had mentally unhinged them and a certain set of circumstances could spark off another series of fits amongst them.

When Louis XIV ascended the French throne he initiated laws to abolish trials for witchcraft. Belief in witches was irrational and this was the age of reason. Louis was deeply shocked by the revelation in 1680 that Madame de Montespan took part in child-murders and Black Mass celebrations in order to retain the love of the king. The royal mistress was said to have laid naked on a black altar with a chalice resting on her stomach. A child's throat was cut and the blood flowed into the chalice; the body was then thrown into an oven. When the king heard this story he dismissed Madame de Montespan.

Yet for all his rationalism the Sun King seems to have had the palace of Versailles built to an occult plan. The ascent from the rear, where all the classical deities were represented in the fountains and groves, led by stages to a staircase beside the royal theatre and up by a long gallery to the Hall of Mirrors. This hall is decorated with a superabundance of relief masks of the great god Pan. It was rumoured in the seventeenth century that the Hall of Mirrors was the scene of ritual magic on a grand scale – ceremonies which involved naked participants of the highest rank. Nor were these harmless romps of the sort

left The Rose and the honey bees. A symbol of the Rosicrucian Society, designed by Robert Fludd in 1626.
below The discovery of the uncorrupted body of Christian Rosenkreuz in 1604 by members of the Third Order of the Rosicrucians. It was said that Rosenkreuz died in 1484.

below Bronze astrological pendant giving the concordances of the days of the week with planetary influences with the alchemical qualities of the metals associated with them. (Seventeenth century.)

painted by Boucher, but rather a ritual means of uniting the powers of heaven and earth – a mixture of Christianity and classical lore typical of the period. The king felt that he was in no way compromising his Catholic beliefs, but that he was ensuring the welfare of France.

While Europe was moving away from witch-fever the disease was just breaking in the New World. Just as the Roman legions carried their military cults to the hinterlands of the empire so did the Pilgrims bring to New England their witch-prejudice and nurture it there with laws carrying the death penalty for offenders. In Massachusetts and Connecticut in 1692 the last great outbreak of witch-fever

among civilized people was experienced.

Some of the settlers around Salem owned slaves who had been transported north from the West Indies. Among them was a young woman from Barbados named Tituba. From an interpretation of the trial evidence it seems she used to indulge in a gentle spirit-cult now known as Pocomania. Several of the village girls at Salem found the ritual dances and rhythmic songs very attractive, and like Tituba they began to fall into trances. The girls, about eight of them to begin with, ranged in age from eleven to twenty. They met in secret with Tituba. The two youngest, however, Abigail aged twelve and Ann aged eleven suddenly developed strange fits, howling, rolling about and crawling

below Reconstruction of a scene in the convent at Loudun, France. The nuns became victims of induced devil-possession, allegedly under the influence of the local priest, Urban Grandier. From the Warner Bros film 'The Devils', 1971.

below right A demonstration before an audience interested in the scientific study of natural phenomena; in this case, the behaviour of liquids. London 1748.

on all fours like animals. The villagers of Salem, replete with Old World superstitions, concluded that the Devil had possessed the two children. In February 1692 the girls had recovered sufficiently to accuse Tituba and two other white women, whom they and their friends disliked, of having caused their pains. An enquiry was held and the three accused women were confronted by the girls who immediately at the sight of them fell into convulsive fits. Tituba – perhaps in revenge for the cruelties of slavery – began to implicate several other settlers as witch-tormentors of the children. Panic seized the community and a court under the auspices of the Governor of the Colony, Sir William Phipps, was held. Again the children fell into animal trances when faced with the supposed witches. The court took this as evidence enough to hang several women. The Governor returned to England and the case continued in other hands. The two girls' fits continued and in an orgy of accusation they cast suspicion on, among others, the Governor's wife and the President of Harvard University. Governor Phipps returned from England in 1693

to call a halt to the excesses and when the dust settled the tally read twenty people hanged, fifty-five tortured and hundreds of innocent men and women imprisoned, or fled into exile.

Cotton Mather, the Presbyterian divine of Boston, a voluminous writer and obdurate believer in witches, wrote much about these cases. He concluded that the persecutions had purged the village of Salem, which had been itself the victim of a Satanic assault. The mystery remains: did Abigail and Ann become genuinely inspired and through some evil post-hypnotic suggestion accuse their innocent neighbours? Or did they calculate the whole affair between them, at first simulating trances and fits in order to draw attention to themselves and indulge in some malicious fun at the expense of Tituba, then getting carried away by their own hysteria, accusing anyone whose name they could remember? Whatever the explanation, the case of the witches of Salem ended all trials for witchcraft in America.

Sir William Phipps must have noticed a great disparity between the self-righteous bigotry of the Puritan ethic in

right A ceremony for descrying the future through images seen in a bowl of liquid. The room is decorated with 'hieroglyphical' symbols. From the 'Thrice Holy Trinosophie' of the Comte de St Germain.
below A reconstruction of a toast to the demonic powers by members of the Hell Fire Club in the chalk caves at West Wycombe, Buckinghamshire, England.
far right Animal Magnetism or Hypnotism. The operator is shown projecting the 'influence' on his patient. Early nineteenth century.

pursuit of witches (as embodied in such luminaries as Cotton Mather), and the comparatively tolerant attitudes he would have encountered in the England of 1692. The rock-like certainties on which the Plymouth Brethren had founded their faith were no longer shared by the Old World. The dawning of the new age of culture and classical learning had tempted the official clergy away from the more tiresome disciplines of their office, especially in England. The eighteenth century was the age of the fox-hunting parson who loved his food and drink. The peasantry and poor labourers in the growing towns might derive some amusement at least from the scurrilous caricatures of debauchery in ecclesiastical circles by artists like Hogarth, Gilray and Rowlandson.

This was the age of Casanova and the Wig Club, an age of irreligious fun for the intellectuals who indulged not only in erotic adventurism but in rather morbid anti-religious ceremonials. It was fashionable to re-enact legends of the demonic past for amusement, though some groups took it more seriously and hoped to conjure up power as well. Some of the more sprightly escapades centered around the manor of Medmenham, beside the Thames near Henley, and its young owner, Lord Dash-wood, who created the Hell Fire Club (much less diabolic than its counterpart in Ireland!).

The aristocratic members of the club gathered at Medmenham dressed as monks and nuns. They sang bawdy hymns to Satan and conducted imitation religious services. This was all a prelude to an orgy around the altar table with naked actresses in attendance. Between 1750 and 1763 Lord Dashwood had caves dug through a hill on the estate with a chamber carved out beside an underground stream. This chamber was used for some secret ceremony although the dampness and chilly atmosphere precluded the possibility of nakedness and eroticism here. Other rites were performed in the ruined abbey in the grounds; once a guest nearly died of fright when a tame black ape leapt on his back. But otherwise little harm was done and eventually the order melted away as its young members began to accept the responsibility of their high birth to become politicians – too busy and soon too old for such carnal pastimes.

The drunken and licentious escapades of the Hell Fire Club were remarkably frivolous compared with the serious-ness of purpose with which Count Alexandro Cagliostro pursued the occult arts and exercised his healing powers. Born in Palermo in 1743, his real name was Giuseppe Balsamo. After a criminal and dissolute youth he travelled in the east, where he studied alchemy. He then wandered about Europe with his wife Serafina selling love philtres and drugs, and acquired a great reputation as a healer. (Amongst the bogus count's various fraudulent claims was the offer of everlasting youth to anyone who could pay the price of his secret.)

He and his wife turned up in London in 1776, and as a Freemason Cagliostro was welcomed by his fellow masons and accepted into the best society. He involved himself deeply in alchemical experiments and studied the inner meaning of Pythagorean numerical magic. He introduced Swedenborgian mysticism to the Lodges and made himself extremely popular by predicting winners on the sweep-stakes. (Even so, on one visit to London he ended up in the Fleet prison for a time.) In Paris he quickly gained a reputation for miraculous healing powers, presumably in connection with his alchemical experiments.

Unfortunately for Cagliostro and his wife they became implicated in the scandal surrounding Marie Antoinette's diamond necklace (the Countess de Lamotte had cheated a royal jeweller of a necklace worth £85,000 on the pretence that Queen Marie Antoinette had consented to buy it) and though proved innocent Cagliostro left France under duress. He returned to England, where he wrote a pamphlet predicting the downfall of the French monarchy and the storming of the Bastille. On a visit to Rome his wife denounced him as a heretic and he was seized by the Papal guard and brought to trial for devil-worship and theft. Though condemned to death his sentence was commuted to life imprisonment – in a cell below ground level in perpetual darkness. There he died in 1795, strangled, it is said, by a sympathetic jailer who spared him years of wasting away. Serafina was exiled to a convent in Poland where later she died unhappily. She and her husband were to be among the last victims of the Inquisition.

Another mysterious figure who prophesied the French Revolution was le Comte de St Germaine – only he is said to have done so when he made an appearance after his death in 1784! He also foretold the rise of Napoleon Bonaparte. It was believed that he had lived for over two thousand years. Science had no response to such beliefs other than to dismiss them out of hand.

With the arrival of the nineteenth century, if Napoleon was emperor of half Europe then science was king of the world, and the new pretender was not going to lose its crown to old outmoded ideas and superstitions. Electricity had been harnessed and Benjamin Franklin had shattered the ancient mystery of lightning by proving that it was

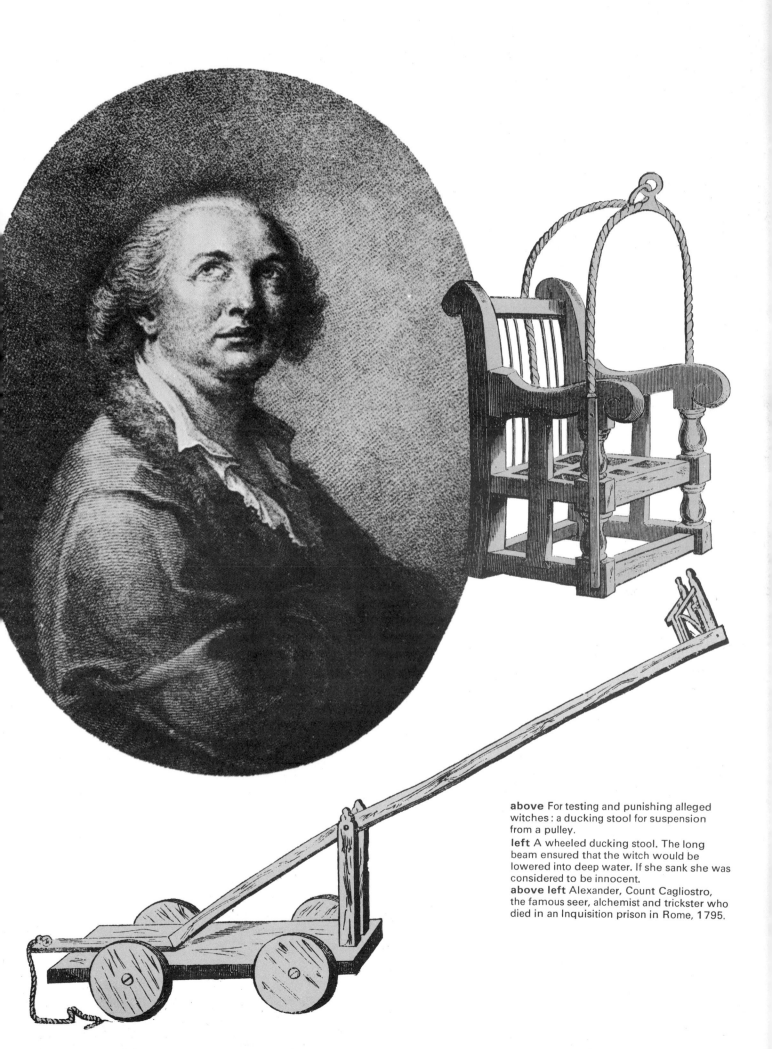

above For testing and punishing alleged witches: a ducking stool for suspension from a pulley.

left A wheeled ducking stool. The long beam ensured that the witch would be lowered into deep water. If she sank she was considered to be innocent.

above left Alexander, Count Cagliostro, the famous seer, alchemist and trickster who died in an Inquisition prison in Rome, 1795.

left The modern world of science and technology : the forces of nature harnessed to serve mankind The ironworks at Rheinhausen, Germany.
above A modern survival of the ancient fertility dances of May Day. The traditional Furry Dance of Helston, Cornwall.

caused by the discharge of electricity. The Austrian physician Friedrich Mesmer had patented his Mesmeric bath in Paris and was using electric shocks to stimulate his patients to health. One of his followers, a certain Marquis de Puysegur employed a non-electrical method of calming patients by gazing into their eyes and making 'Mesmeric passes' with his hands. The system worked and the treatment (which was thought of as magic, since there was no explanation for it) became very popular, much to the anger of the orthodox medical fraternity throughout Europe.

Yet for all the new knowledge and technology, magic still bubbled away happily, whether as peasant superstition or as amusing diversion for bored aristocrats. In Napoleon's

court the beautiful West Indian Empress Josephine was well schooled in her island's magic, though she was less sophisticated perhaps than the court's star occultist, Mademoiselle Marie Lenormand, 'the Sybil of the Faubourg Saint-Germain'. This clairvoyant had amazing powers of prediction; she read in the cards of the impending divorce of the empress.

After the Napoleonic wars the new technology was applied to the business of living: communications were established through Europe with canals and roads. New industrial cities sprang up near natural resources; mining towns and mill towns were everywhere. But the workers who inhabited these new urban complexes were country folk transplanted. To the towns they brought the old dances and songs of the agricultural festivals, and their fertility processions – anything to alleviate the appalling conditions of industrial life and bring a little gaiety to the round of back-breaking work in the mines and the factories. This obeisance to the new god Progress blinded the emergent capitalist class to the plight of the human beings who made the system work. It took a mystic visionary like William Blake to see the condition of humanity enslaved by the machines they thought they operated. In censuring the 'dark Satanic mills' Blake was not just denouncing the grim factories and the debasement of the men and women who sweated long hours inside them; he was trying to open people's eyes to a real and dangerous threat of spiritual evil.

Blake was fifteen years old when the philosopher and visionary Emanuel Swedenborg died in 1772 but the religion of love and the ascent towards God which Swedenborg had taught resembled the teachings of Blake and his circle. According to the Swedish philosopher's theosophic system, God, as Divine Man, is infinite love and infinite wisdom, from whom the two worlds of nature and spirit emanate, separate but closely related. The work of other devout religious philosophers like Jakob Böhme and Freiherr furthered this idea of a link between Man and the great Architect of the Universe. Not everyone in the nineteenth century bowed down before the steel god of progress; some poets and philosophers stood firm for the things of the spirit.

At the time of Waterloo most Englishmen still worked on the land or were connected with agricultural trades; but by 1830 half the population were to become town-dwellers engaged in industry. Although separated from the soil they clung affectionately to the old country festivals as a welcome escape from the Dickensian horrors of the industrial slums. The mill and pit owners had in the main little concern for the welfare of their workers, whatever their age, as long as wages were kept low and hours long.

Drink was the opiate of this disadvantaged class whose drunkenness on pay-night appalled the prospering middle classes living around them. Undismayed, the slum-dwellers enlived their dreary streets with processions to honour Jack-in-the-Green; they chose their Queen of the May and the small boys begged for pennies around the burning guy or beside little grottoes built of shells and leaves as shrines to St James of Compostella. These old country customs, transplanted into the towns, became a kind of gentle saturnalia.

While the poor paid their pennies to the gipsy fortune-tellers at the fairs and pier ends, the prosperous tradesmen and their wives had recourse to Madam Clairvoyante. In that age of visible change and material progress people of all walks of life were uncertain about the future, and the result was a sudden passion for fortune-telling. A practice once condemned as witchery became a fashionable diversion. The cards and tea cups were read as avidly below stairs as they were above – and if what was revealed came to pass the cards were blamed, not the telepathic power of the medium, since little was known or understood about the unconscious levels of the mind.

Although the same social patterns existed in America at the beginning of the nineteenth century, there were some who took the supernatural more seriously. In the small town of Sharon in Vermont State, Joseph Smith had a vision in 1820 ordering him to become a prophet of the Most High for the purpose of restoring the Gospel. Three years later an angel named Moroni told him where to find a book written on plates of gold. With the book Smith

Chapter Seven

Magic IN AN *Urban Landscape*

found two stones which helped him to decipher its message. The existence of this book of gold was sworn to by trustworthy witnesses.

The angel appeared once more and took back the book from Smith, who at the time was in the company of some hard-headed local businessmen. They shared his vision and gave their sworn testimony to the reality of the angel. Joseph Smith founded in 1831 the Church of Jesus Christ of the Latter-day Saints, and his small community settled eventually in Illinois. But far from being sanctified for his angelic visitations he was subjected to the obloquy of the mob because of disorders resulting from internal dissension in his groups. Accused thirty times in courts of law, Smith was eventually assassinated by a gang of ruffians while in prison at Carthage, Illinois. His successor Brigham Young, a carpenter, led a group of faithful followers out west fifteen hundred miles to the banks of the Great Salt Lake in the Utah desert, surviving a murderous attack by militia en route. There they founded Salt Lake City as the home of the Mormon religion.

In England as early as 1837 some two thousand people were converted to the Church of Latter-day Saints. Today the great worldwide organization, the Mormon Church, has millions of followers who lead a sober, God-fearing life, practising a religion which began with a strange apparition to an unremarkable man in Vermont State more than a hundred and fifty years ago.

The existence of ghosts was to the educated minds of the nineteenth century something of a superstition; but the experiences of the Fox family of Hydesville, New York, seriously challenged that attitude. Their small house had for some time echoed with the sound of thuds and rattlings in the night. On 31 March 1848, the Foxes' young daughters Kate and Margaret entered into the spirit of things by knocking on the wall to see if the 'ghost' would knock back. It was claimed that they did in fact establish communication by means of rapping and learnt that a pedlar had been murdered there and buried in a shallow grave in the garden. Much later some human remains were discovered in the place indicated by the ghostly messages. The Hydesville rappings caused a sensation and the Fox family had to move away to escape the curious crowds.

left Jack-in-the-Green with his companions, the Clown, Maid Marion, the West Indians and two chimney sweeps, dance on May Day. Detail from painting *c.* 1820.

Later the two girls were persuaded to give demonstrations of table-rapping and their success sparked off a popular craze both in America and Britain for psychical phenomena.

The craze gained momentum in 1852 from the arrival in Britain of the medium Mrs Hayden, who claimed to be able to contact people's relatives beyond the grave. The mushrooming cult attracted many charlatans who were exposed from time to time – like the bearded gentleman who was caught in a flash photo with a shawl round his head and his trousers down! But in spite of the frequent frauds the idea of spiritualism caught on. Its practice depended upon the presence of mediums, those individuals who could disassociate from their normal personality to become a receptacle through which disembodied spirits could manifest themselves.

Sometimes the medium would speak in a tongue unknown to him or be seen to levitate and float through the air. Some mediums released a tangible emanation from their bodies known as ectoplasm which took on human form and features, occasionally detaching itself completely. The most notable example of this was an extremely solid ghost called Katie King who was written up by the great physicist Professor William Crookes – although the charming Katie is now thought to be a fraud (one of the professor's girl friends in fancy dress).

Other ghostly personages are not so easily explained away. For instance the ectoplasmic images projected by Eusapia Palladino. This great Sicilian medium transmitted portraits of the deceased president of France on a screen of ectoplasmic draperies. Eventually this recurrent image was traced to a newspaper photograph Eusapia had seen as a little girl. Did she project a forgotten image from her own subconscious or did the president of France choose to manifest himself through her?

One remarkable aspect of spiritualism was the apparent generation of power and movement independent of any physical agency. People seated around a table might have caused it to rock and even to tap out messages but could not have lifted it clean into the air without visible means of support. During some sessions individuals were actually levitated in much the same manner as Saint Teresa of Avila. In London on 16 December 1868 the famous medium Daniel Dunglass Home surprised a group of socialites by floating to the ceiling, flying out of an upper storey window and in by another after a short trip over the pavement near Hyde Park. Questioned about his night flight Home repeated the performance which he said was carried out on instructions from the actress Ada Mencken

below A table-tapping seance in the 1870s. Even under a harsh light the table mover inexplicably taps out messages from beyond the grave.
right Drawing of a charlatan medium. The head is a libellous likeness of the famous occultist D. D. Home who was lampooned by his enemies as 'Mr Sludge the Medium'.
below right A posed 'ghost' photograph around 1890. Note the retouching of the garden border through the sheeted 'spectre'.

above Sir William Crookes, the eminent physicist (1834–1919). A founder of the Society for Psychical Research. His scientific study of apparitions produced evidence of their physical reality. He has, however, recently been accused of fraud in the case of the 'ghost' of Katie King.

who had died a few months before. Daniel Dunglass Home differed from the traditional message-giving medium in being acted upon by a psycho-kinetic force of great power; in a more primitive society he would have been esteemed as a great shaman.

To the scientific mind the whole business of spiritualism was incomprehensible. Evidence could not be evaluated nor tests applied and to complicate matters most of the mediums were really like primitive shamans. These gentle people were often completely out of touch with every-day realities and were suggestible to such a degree that they sincerely believed their own abilities to produce their strange phenomena. Because so many of their number resorted to trickery and extortion it was easy to throw a blanket condemnation over their ranks.

If the search for the supernatural was an amusing diversion for the rich it was something of a necessity for the poor – like alcohol, a means of escape from the work-prison of their everyday life. For this reason religious movements proliferated, attracting the working man who joined the congregation to satisfy his spiritual hunger. In America groups like the Shakers, with their puritanical credo coupled with ecstatic dances, boomed in the 1860s, perhaps because of the menace of the Civil War. In Britain, although there was a tradition of religious revivalism from the time of Wesley's Nonconformist Church, there was no longer the zealousness that had once supported the reformers. So the new social conditions spawned many evangelical sects of which the most powerful was the Salvation Army, since it filled the stomachs of the poor before preaching to them.

The social and religious impact of the Salvation Army was – and still is – enormous. One of their particular 'magics' was to borrow the popular melodies of bawdy music-hall ballads for the singing of Christian hymns – a shrewd tactic employed by the founder General William Booth who reputedly defended himself by saying, 'Why should the Devil have all the best tunes?'

With the rise of compulsory education all children had the opportunity of knowledge hitherto reserved for those able to afford it. Yet the Godivas still rode on May Day, modestly clothed however, and the sweeps collected pennies in the guise of Jack-in-the-Green. Although there was a lingering fear of witches in remoter areas nobody paid much attention to them other than young boys who might torment a surly old woman who lived alone. For the country folk the strict pattern of church attendance was the solid basis of life's routine and they had no knowledge

left Sir Oliver Lodge, physicist and co-founder of the Society for Psychical Research. His book 'Raymond' dealt with posthumous messages from his son who had been killed in World War I.
below Ecstatic inspiration in a Christian congregation. The final procession of a Shaker meeting. The participants feel themselves to have been inspired by the Holy Spirit.

right The white-haired Mrs Annie Besant (1847–1933), leader of the Theosophical movement, with the young Krishnamurti and other Indian and British friends of the Order of the Star of the East.
far right Annie Besant in her late teens (*c.* 1865), already revealing her deeply introspective and understanding personality.
below Mormon missionaries baptising American Indians, 1882.

below The Mormon Temple, Salt Lake City, Utah: the heart of the faith. The building conforms to the biblical measurements of Solomon's Temple in Jerusalem.

above Mrs Bone: one of the leading
exponents of the Old Religion, with the
September offering of first fruits at a
prehistoric stone circle in Cumberland.
below A modern witch priestess
wearing only her ceremonial necklace
welcomes a new initiate into the coven.
Note the ceremonial knives on the low altar
in the foreground.

turned this very capable man to the pursuit of mysticism
as a deliberate rejection of the social and moral custom of
his day. He went as far as celebrating an equivalent of
witch ceremonials, using the sexual element not as a
tension-builder but as an erotic part of the ceremony itself.

Crowley attracted a good many followers. They held
their ceremonies at the magical Abbey of Theleme, but
eventually the organization of the secret society collapsed.
Even without his followers Crowley tried to be as evil as
he could out of sheer perversity. Scornful of Christianity,
he tried to substitute his own religion of sexual magic. Yet
for all this he was a likeable man, and retained many friends
up to the time of his death who were present at his bizarre
funeral. Crowley's writings and the religion he named after
himself are much studied today: as we have seen, whenever
humanity experiences a period of confusion and tension the
occult path becomes more attractive.

Crowley was by nature a self-publicist who drew as much
attention to himself and his beliefs as he could. But other
practitioners of black magic were much more circumspect;

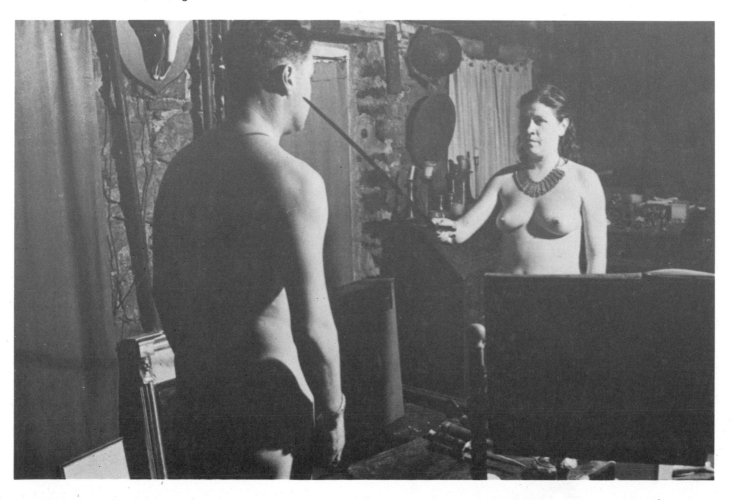

left Gerald Brousseau Gardner, founder of a group of witch covens in Britain. These groups based their practices partly on old English traditions and partly on Etruscan traditions preserved in Leland's 'Aradia'. below The Adamites of Amsterdam: an ecstatic religious group of the seventeenth century. They believed that worship should be conducted in the nude – as many modern witches do. As non-conformists they were subjected to much persecution and were eventually suppressed.

they courted no publicity and their activities never leaked out. They held secret meetings in which ritual magic was employed for destructive purposes. By their very nature such cults were usually confined to very small groups.

The Theosophical Society had laid the groundwork for a

growing number of movements in the first half of the twentieth century which studied oriental and transcendental philosophy and religion; the Zen Buddhists, the Sūfi Order, the Christian Scientists, and many other smaller groups. Their common belief was the need for mankind to find its inner self – the soul, capable of communing with its creator. Some of these groups were deits, some were not, but all sought a way to holiness. (The most modern exponent of this concept is the Maharishi Mahesh, who in 1972 was recruited to teach transcendental meditation to members of the United States Army.) These modern mystics were much influenced by eighteenth-century mystics like William Blake, whose works they reprinted.

Too often we forget that these struggles towards an understanding of metaphysical realities coincided with great trauma for mankind, at times when the pattern of his life was rent by fratricidal wars or violent social upheaval. Out of the miseries and frustrations of the late nineteenth century emerged new concepts of medicine. Freud showed us how people torment themselves with suppressed emotions which surface in their consciousness in a distorted form. Jung postulated that all of us, sane or unbalanced, have within us a series of archetypal ideas which bear striking similarities to the myths of our ancestors, a kind of primitive religion surviving within the human personality. Jung suggested that it was this aspect of our inner self which functions in strange religious outbursts at times of great crisis, when the unexpected memory of ancient rituals returns. Of this sort would be the rituals enacted by witch-covens of recent times.

Psychoanalysis, for those who could afford it, became an escape route in times of crisis, performing the same function for the rich as the revivalist religions of the masses; the fundamental desire for happiness expressed itself in these pursuits. Its most vigorous expression was probably in the bible-punching revivalism of the 1920s. Hot Gospellers like Aimée Semple Macpherson whipped up their congregations to a religious fervour. People flocked to her meetings to confess their sinfulness and seek salvation much as they do for the Reverend Billy Graham today. Some groups like the Southern Baptists sought religious expression in ecstasy. Others took a different road; the Seventh Day Adventists for instance regulated all their activities with puritanical zeal. But this need for primitive religious emotion in times of despair showed that the orthodox churches did not fill the void.

Apart from the exotic cults which mushroomed as a result of violently changing social structures in Europe and

HEMOSTOPILÉ

upper A magic circle. Within its circumference the practitioners are protected from dangerous spirit powers. The inscription refers to the names of God in Latin, Greek and Hebrew.

above The Seal symbol of Hemostophile: if called upon by these signs he can compel demons to reveal themselves. Such ritual symbols are characteristic of late eighteenth-century ceremonial magic.

right A gathering of the Ku Klux Klan, a secret society formed during the American Civil War, dedicated to white Protestant supremacy in America. The colour of the robes marks the position of members in the hierarchy.

below A doll used in telepathic magic for destructive purposes. It is shrouded and placed in a coffin – symbolic of the desired fate for its victim.
lower right Charles Manson, a modern self-confessed Satanist, accused of ritual murder in California in 1970.

America between the wars, witchcraft and forms of Satanism began to thrive again. Another curious development was the nudist movement which began simply with little groups of people who shed their clothes on sunny afternoons. The movement shocked the sensibilities of the 1930s and naturists were persecuted for their 'immoral' ways. Persecution gave Naturism a cultist feeling especially since most of its proponents were vegetarians and committed to the healthy outdoor life and exercise. A history of popular antipathy left its stamp on the movement by making Naturists so defensive that their rules of moral conduct became rigidly puritanical.

One of the less happy aspects of the early nudist cults was the division in Germany – the homeland of the movement – into two antipathetic groups: the nature-worshippers who held that all men were equal under the sun (a philosophy counter to Aryanism), and a minority who sought to revive Nordic paganism. The racist nature of these latter groups ensured their survival in Nazi Germany, although nudity was not encouraged by the regime, who funnelled youthful exuberance into the heavily clothed 'Strength through Joy' movement, and anyone suspected of having links with the free-thinking nudists was branded as a Gipsy or a Jew. The period of tension before the Second World War, and the apocalyptic destruction of cities which followed, gave a tremendous impetus to the growth of occultism of all kinds. Seers bilked distraught parents of

those who 'sacrificed to demons, destroyed other people by spells, or used divinations of devilish witchcrafts'. For some covens it made little difference since they believed themselves to be outside the law anyway. The repeal of this outdated act was supposed to express the belief that witchcraft did not exist; in fact it opened the way for public demonstrations by many esoteric religious groups. The idea of women learning to be witches sounded laughable to the public mind, and its seriousness was further undermined when the mass media filled their pages with salacious tales of naked ceremonies and erotic initiation rites.

The cult spread, however, and members of covens broke away to become leaders of their own groups. They were cautious about new postulants, who were frequently put through some amusing exercises and gradually edged out of the society if they were found to be psychologically unsuitable. The old textbooks on witchcraft were re-edited and frequently other cults were grafted on, particularly the cult of Isis which appealed to the mind of the 1930s.

An important group of covens formed around the late Gerald Brousseau Gardner. The rituals followed by these covens were somewhat confused since their leader had introduced into traditional witchcraft a great deal of the magical ceremonies of the Sea Gipsies, which he had picked up during his many years in Malaya. Gardner's adaptations of ritual for Britain were based on Leland's book *Aradia*, though for a long time he managed to conceal the plagiarism. A man with a sense of fun as well as a deep knowledge of occultism, he attracted a considerable following. In later life Gardner set out to popularize witchcraft and his warm personality as much as his naked rituals spread his fame. Though dismissed by purists, the Gardner covens still exist, even if rival groups dispute their powers.

A not infrequent occurrence in our days is the sight of witches of various persuasions arguing their case on television. And if the sight of witches in our living-rooms excites the imagination, there are museums in the Isle of Man and in Cornwall where the curious can learn more about their practices, and in particular how to distinguish between the two main groups: witchcraft as nature-worship and the witchcraft of ceremonial magicians. (The former invariably perform their rituals in the open air and dance outside their magic circle, whereas the latter conjure their magic indoors, inside a circle.)

The rituals of ceremonial magic are not always healthy, as stories of Satanist sects, black sorcery and sadistic practices attest. Evidence of diabolism can be seen in the wrecking of Christian symbols, the desecration of cemeteries

above A demonstration of ceremonial magic. The 'Devil' of the coven traditionally preached the black sermon while the priestess exercised the magical power. The pentagram in the background with one point downwards is a symbol of female power.
right The charming of a wax doll. A spell is cast on the doll which becomes an instrument of destructive magic. The will is expressed by the 'Devil' and the intention by the knife of the priestess.

large fees for tracing missing soldiers, mostly by using pendulum divination over a map of Europe. Spiritists were kept busily employed seeking news of the dead, and frequently brought consolation. One group of English witches claimed to have made Hitler abandon his plans for a cross-channel invasion by performing a sacrificial ritual.

In 1951 the Witchcraft Act was finally removed from the British statute book – a law which stretched back to the year 690 when Theodore of Canterbury legislated against

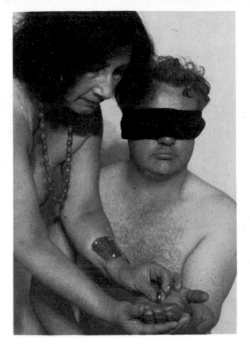

and occasional ritual murders. In south Germany around 1960 there was a group of thrill-seeking young people who hunted and decapitated deer for a blood-drinking rite. When arrested they turned out to be a group of young socialites escaping the boredom of their lives by the pursuit of the esoteric!

Even more macabre were the circumstances surrounding the Moors Murders in Britain. At the time of the trial of Myra Hindley and Ian Brady in 1967 the most sickening photographs and film strips of child-torture were circulating. In America the Manson trial revealed the existence to the world of a Church of Satan and its penchant for ritual murder. Only when such horrific events come to light do we realize the existence of black magic societies in our midst. Black Mass is celebrated today, and just as the Voodoo priests bite into the necks of chickens in an ecstatic blood-letting ritual, so do the celebrants sacrifice a live animal and collect its blood.

If Apuleius' intelligent ass were to wander through the western world today he would find us as magic-crazy as his own decadent Roman Empire. There is no practice mentioned in *The Golden Ass* which could not be found in our society. Even to the savage cruelties staged in the name of entertainment – although ours are simulated on celluloid in films like *The Straw Dogs* and *The Devils*, instead of being real combats in the gladiatorial ring. The popularity of another film, *Rosemary's Baby*, with its ideas of incubus and Devil-worship shows our modern fascination with witchcraft; and the lucky charms we carry – are these not palpable evidence of our superstitions?

The great 'Is-God-dead?' debate of the 1960s has shown that orthodox religion has had to accept a minority role in the conduct of human affairs. Even in Catholic countries, where a traditional Church-and-State link still exists and religion remains strong, there is a move towards ecumenicity. This means of inter-group toleration offers a divided Christian Church the defence of coming together on its common ground to face the challenge of secularism.

As the star of orthodox religion wanes, that of the occult waxes. All the evidence points to a growing interest in the more popular manifestations of witchcraft: the use of charms, the reading of horoscopes and the interpretation of dreams. In spite of the media's suspicion of esoteric societies and their practices, the supernatural offers a flight from the nuts-and-bolts preoccupations of science and its uncompromising certainties. If science informs us that all matter is merely a series of vortices in space and that we are no more than a combination of electrical charges, what then is Truth?

above The symbol of acceptance. An initiate is given a ring to welcome him into the coven. The silver and amber worn by the High Priestess are symbolic materials linked with ancient astrological beliefs. **below** The Maharishi Mahesh teaching his religious philosophy of universal love to a gathering of his followers in India.

above A witches' wedding : members of the coven and their 'Devil' in romantic costume raise their hands in blessing.
below Maharishi Mahesh, the Indian guru whose teaching of universal gentleness has had a great influence on young people today.

right Midsummer meditation. Crowned with daisies and ivy a young man seeks spiritual enlightenment at the Glastonbury Festival in England.

below The Glastonbury Gathering,
Midsummer 1971. Young people from many
nations camped near the ancient holy sites
at Glastonbury. There was continuous
music from the scale model of the Great
Pyramid.

All through history magic has kept one pace ahead of science. As man's knowledge advances so his imagination takes a greater leap forward. As science explodes the mystery of our universe, breaking it down into atomic diagrams and symbolic equations, so we seek for new wonders in the higher realms of existence. Both America and Russia are currently experimenting with telepathy and clairvoyance in their national interest, investing occultism with political significance. At the same time the ancient temptation of using occult ritual to obtain power and wealth remains.

The more science encroaches on the freedom of the individual – one has only to read Huxley's *Brave New World* to see how many of his doomridden prophesies have come to pass – the more mankind turns towards nature, and particularly the wildwood of ancient times. The desire to create nature-reserves to combat the industrial colossus is not so much a dramatic call for a halt to progress as a demand for simplicity. Young people today are opting out of the industrial system and forming communes close to the land. They have shed the inhibitions that closed like shackles on their forefathers when they moved into the towns at the time of the Industrial Revolution. The whole pop culture with its concommitant nudity – at open-air concerts, on stage and film – will eventually seep down into the basic lifestyle of the western world. Nakedness in terms of today's youth is not a return to eroticism, rather the opposite: a return to the magic of nature.

above Two young people at Glastonbury spontaneously express their feeling of peace and happiness, their bodies attuned to nature around them.

INDEX

PICTURE CREDITS

The Editors gratefully acknowledge the courtesy of the following photographers, publishers, institutions, agencies and corporations for the illustrations in this volume.

or interest in the religious revivals and curious sects that sprang up among the workers and the idle rich. But in every village there was now a school, and the cobwebbed superstitions of country life were gradually being swept away by the arrogant notion that everything could be explained by science.

But when it came to the supernatural there were things that could not be measured, events that could not be repeated in controlled experiment. A new way of looking at such phenomena had to be found where rational analysis failed. Many intellectuals of the late nineteenth and early twentieth centuries turned to the religions of the east. The old mystery traditions of the Celts were forgotten and the western tradition of ritual magic was neglected (except by the Golden Dawn movement, which is mentioned below) for eastern transcendentalism.

Interest in oriental mysticism was stimulated by two women, Helena Blavatsky and her former pupil Annie Besant. Through the study of Hindu and Buddhist teachings, which involved meditation, music and exercises, they sought a higher plane of being, a holy Absolute. The Theosophical Society, founded in New York in 1875 by Madame Blavatsky, Mrs Besant and others, opened a world to its members outside the bounds of science where they could come to a knowledge of God by means of intuition and contemplative illumination.

As the nineteenth century gave way to our own, freedom became the watchword: freedom for the workers and their trade unions, freedom in poetry from traditional forms, freedom on stage for playwrights and freedom in art as expressed by the exotic elegance of *L'Art Nouveau* and its German equivalent *Jugendstil*. The arts reflected a changing world. The *fin de siècle* decadence embodied by Oscar Wilde suffered under the harsh light of modernity; the etiolated eroticism of Aubrey Beardsley's drawing was symptomatic of the decline and disorientation that ended in the disaster of a global war. In the occultist world secret groups convened to practise ritual and kabbalistic magic. The Order of the Golden Dawn for instance, as outlined in the writings of Dion Fortune, based itself on the western occult tradition, though it appears to have been more than just a revival of Celtic beliefs and had abandoned the primitive aspects of sacrifice, relying much more on symbolism, incantation and prayer.

Another aspect of occultism centred around the notorious Aleistair Crowley (1875–1947) who coined the term Crowleianity for his professed creed. A repressed childhood